Self-Leadership:
Determinants and Outcomes

Sevgin Batuk Turan

Self-Leadership: Determinants and Outcomes

PETER LANG

Bibliographic Information published by the Deutsche Nationalbibliothek
The Deutsche Nationalbibliothek lists this publication in the Deutsche
Nationalbibliografie; detailed bibliographic data is available online at
http://dnb.d-nb.de.

Library of Congress Cataloging-in-Publication Data
A CIP catalog record for this book has been applied for at the Library of Congress.

ISBN 978-3-631-74622-6 (Print) · E-ISBN 978-3-631-75300-2 (E-PDF)
E-ISBN 978-3-631-75301-9 (EPUB) · E-ISBN 978-3-631-75302-6 (MOBI)
DOI 10.3726/b13844

Table of Contents

Acknowledgements 7

Chapter 1: Introduction...9

Chapter 2: Self-leadership 13
2.1 Historical development of self-leadership 13
2.2 Self-leadership 15

Chapter 3: Study 1 – Quantitative exploration of
determinants and outcomes of self-leadership 19
3.1 Literature review 19
    3.1.1 Transformational leadership... 19
    3.1.2 High-performance work systems.. 20
    3.1.3 Proactive personality 22
    3.1.4 Work engagement 23
    3.1.5 Organizational citizenship behavior....................................... 25
    3.1.6 Self-efficacy 26
3.2 Conceptual framework and hypotheses development...........................26
    3.2.1 Theoretical framework 26
    3.2.2 Hypotheses development 29
        3.2.2.1 Determinants of self-leadership 29
        3.2.2.2 Outcomes of self-leadership 32
        3.2.2.3 Mediating role of self-efficacy................................ 33
3.3 Research design and methodology...36
    3.3.1 Sampling and data collection.. 37
    3.3.2 Sample characteristics 37
    3.3.3 Measures... 39
    3.3.4 Reliability and validity of the models 43

3.4 Data analyses and hypotheses testing..47

    3.4.1 Study 1 – Model testing (1).. 48

    3.4.2 Study 1 – Model testing (2).. 49

    3.4.3 Analyses regarding demographics... 53

Chapter 4: Study 2 – Qualitative exploration of determinants and outcomes of self-leadership

**Chapter 4: Study 2 – Qualitative exploration of
determinants and outcomes of self-leadership**..............57

4.1 Research design and methodology...57

    4.1.1 Sampling and data collection.. 58

    4.1.2 Sample characteristics 58

4.2 Results of study 2 59

Chapter 5: Discussion and conclusion..73

5.1 Discussion...73

5.2 Implications 83

5.3 Future research directions 84

5.4 Limitations..85

5.5 Conclusions 86

References...87

Acknowledgements

From the time I was in high school, I wanted to be a part of the academic world. It is thanks to all who have contributed to my dream that I have come this far.

First of all, I am deeply grateful to my dear advisor, Professor Hayat Kabasakal, for her endless support and guidance. As I always say, she has been a second mother to all of her students. I am so lucky that I completed this journey with her. Whenever we thought we had come to a dead end, she always lit the way with her knowledge and wisdom. She is an inspiration and a role model for all of us, and I hope we can be worthy of her efforts throughout our lives.

I am indebted to Professor Kıvanç İnelmen and Professor Burcu Rodopman for being in my supervisory committee from the very beginning. I would like to express my sincere thanks for their valuable contributions and advice at every step of the way. They always asked the right questions and opened up new perspectives for me. Without them, this journey would never have been so pleasant and beneficial.

I owe thanks to my committee members, Professor Esin Can and Professor Güler İslamoğlu, for their valuable contributions and suggestions. I am so glad and lucky that they have been a part of this work.

I would also like to express my appreciation to Professor Muzaffer Bodur, Professor Güven Alpay and Professor Hakan Özçelik. I am extremely grateful to be one of their students and to have learned so much from them.

I want to thank all my professors and colleagues at the Turkish- German University and Yildiz Technical University for encouraging me all along this way.

I want to express my gratitude to several institutions which have supported me throughout this journey. I would like to thank the Boğaziçi University Research Fund for the support they provided to my dissertation with the project code 11183. I also would like to thank The Scientific and Technological Research Council of Turkey (TÜBİTAK) for the scholarship they provided me for my doctoral studies.

I owe special thanks to my family and close friends for their eternal understanding. Special acknowledgements go to my dear husband, Birol Turan, my mother Filiz Batuk and my father Seyhan Batuk for holding on with me all during these long years of study, and, most of all, for giving me endless love and support.

Chapter 1 Introduction

Since the 1980s, an emerging concept that has grasped the attention of organizational behavior scholars has been "self-leadership". Rooted in social learning theory (Bandura, 1977), self-leadership has been proposed as an instrument for self-control and self-influence in organizational setting (Manz, 1986).

Organizations use supervision and control in order to identify appropriate behavior, to monitor and coordinate behaviors and to reward and punish accordingly (Lawler & Rhode, 1976). Control processes are supposed to involve application of rational and manageable mechanisms in order to influence employees to assure organizational goal-achievement (Manz, 1986). Although these mechanisms have been considered as assurance for corporate success, this view has fallen short to grasp the notion that individuals have their own values, beliefs and self-control systems (Manz, 1979; Manz, 1986). As organizational control systems have performance standards and evaluation mechanisms, individuals also have their own self-generated personal standards and self-evaluation mechanisms in order to reward or punish themselves (Bandura, 1977; Mahoney & Thoresen, 1974; Manz & Sims, 1980). Therefore, organizational control systems fail to reach and shape individual action directly (Manz, 1986). It means that individual self-control systems lie at the very heart of organizational control systems and the effect that organizational control systems bring about is determined by their interaction with individual self-control systems. Therefore, rather than relying on external control, it is essential to recognize and facilitate employees' self-control systems (Manz, 1986). On the other hand, self-control and management do not necessarily mean "no external influence". Self-management strategies are considered as behaviors that require reinforcement to assure maintenance (Kerr & Slocum, 1981; Manz & Sims, 1980; Thoresen & Mahoney, 1974).

In this respect, determining the drivers and facilitators of self-management and self-leadership has become crucial for organizations to achieve envisioned organizational goals. In this book, therefore, these questions are addressed: "What are the contextual triggering mechanisms that activate and increase self leadership skills of employees? Are there any dispositional factors that contribute to self-leadership?" The aim is to identify the dispositional and context-dependent determinants of self-leadership and to explain the importance of this concept by referring to its anticipated outcomes.

To answer these questions, a sequential mixed methodology was applied and two separate studies were conducted. The first study was conducted by survey method. It includes two models regarding different research questions. The second study was conducted via semi-structured in-depth interviews. Mixed methodological designs combine the use of both quantitative and qualitative methods in order to analyze data and are especially preferred in organizational research (Cameron, 2009). In this respect, with the help of this methodology, the results of both studies are expected to complement each other in order to gain a deeper understanding about the antecedents and consequences of self-leadership.

Study 1 consists of the quantitative part of the research and is based on two models. Drawing on self-determination theory, transformational leadership and high-performance work systems (HPWS) are expected to positively affect and facilitate self-leadership skills of employees. Through the satisfaction of the psychological needs of the employees, these two variables are expected to contribute to self-leadership. On the other hand, proactive personality is expected to be a dispositional antecedent of self-leadership. It means that employees who have proactive personality characteristics are expected to exert more self-leadership skills. Therefore, the purpose of the first model is to see if these variables help to stimulate self-leadership skills of employees and to see if contextual or dispositional factors are more likely to explain the variance in self-leadership skills.

In the second model, organizational citizenship behavior (OCB) and work engagement are introduced as possible outcomes of self-leadership and the effect of self-leadership on these anticipated outcomes are investigated. In these relationships, self-leadership is expected to contribute to OCB and work engagement through enhanced self-efficacy. In this respect, the mediator role of self-efficacy is also investigated.

After that, Study 2 is conducted to find out other possible antecedents/blockers and outcomes of self-leadership through in-depth interviews. Through this study, it is expected to open up future research directions for scholars and to deepen and complement the findings of Study 1.

The research questions addressed in this book are summarized below.

RQ1. What are the contextual determinants of self-leadership? Can an external leadership style (transformational leadership) facilitate self-leadership skills?

RQ2. Can a systemic construct, namely high-performance work systems, facilitate self-leadership?

RQ3. Is there a relationship between proactive personality and self-leadership?

RQ4. How does self-leadership affect employee outcomes (Organizational citizenship behavior, work engagement)?

RQ5. What other contextual factors can contribute to/hinder self-leadership skills?

Leadership styles that emphasize participation of employees are considered as necessary tools in facilitating self-leadership, because, this kind of leaders allow employees to exercise influence over work processes (Stewart, Courtright, & Manz, 2011). Especially transformational leadership has been proposed as a leadership style that can enhance self-leadership by encouraging employees to think independently, to develop their own ideas, and to critically question their results (Andressen, Konradt, & Neck, 2012); but the research over the effect of an external leader is very limited. On the other hand, self-leadership research has been intertwined with individual and team level drivers of self-leadership, but, at the organizational level, the research comprises of only training and reward systems. Training and the structure of reward systems have been shown to affect the use of self-leadership strategies (Stewart et al., 2011). In this respect, this research aims to provide a more general framework that integrates training, reward systems, job descriptions, participation, mobility etc. and proposes HPWS as a possible facilitator of self-leadership.

In terms of dispositional factors, studies related with self-leadership have been conducted around Big Five Personality Traits. First hypothesized by Williams (1997) and later empirically investigated by Houghton and colleagues (2004), self-leadership is shown to be correlated with extraversion and conscientiousness of the Big Five Personality Traits. A more recent study conducted by Furtner and Rauthmann (2010) implied a relationship between self-leadership and traits of extraversion and openness to experience. This area still lacks research about different personality traits' effects on self-leadership. Therefore, it is claimed that, proactive personality can be a determinant of self-leadership skills. Proactive personality and self-leadership operate according to the same rationale: controlling the external environment. Therefore, it is expected that, individuals who have proactive personality will be more likely to exert self-leadership skills.

Another area of contribution is job outcomes. Although the main interest is to identify the drivers of self-leadership, showing why this concept is so vital is another area of interest. Therefore, we propose that, self-leadership will have a positive effect on job outcomes such as work engagement and OCB. Previous research has shown that self-leadership is positively related to productivity, job satisfaction, organizational commitment and career success (Stewart et al., 2011). Taking that further, this research aims to see if different positive job outcomes are affected by self-leadership. In a parallel fashion, other positive job behaviors such as engagement and OCB are also expected to increase with the use of self-leadership skills. In this respect, with the help of this conceptualization, it is planned to make contribution to the "job outcomes" literature, too.

Besides these, with the help of the interviews conducted, it is aimed to see whether the answers of the participants provide additional insights to the first study. In addition to that, other factors that can complement the findings of the first study are investigated in order to gain a deeper understanding of possible contextual determinants, inhibitors and outcomes of self-leadership.

This book includes five chapters. In Chapter 2, the history of self-leadership theory and relevant literature on the concept will be presented. In Chapter 3, the quantitative part of the research will be introduced. First of all, the other variables of interest that are investigated through the quantitative study – Study 1 will be explained briefly. Afterwards, the theoretical framework and hypotheses development will be presented and research models of Study 1 will be introduced. The methodology and sample characteristics will be discussed, and finally, data analyses and hypotheses testing for the research models will be given. In Chapter 4, the qualitative part is explained. The methodology and sample characteristics for the qualitative study – Study 2 will be given alongside the results. Finally, in Chapter 5, the findings and limitations of both studies will be discussed and implications will be mentioned along with future research directions.

Chapter 2 Self-leadership

Abstract: In this chapter, the historical development of self-leadership will be summarized and the theoretical foundations will be given.

2.1 Historical development of self-leadership

With the beginning of the 21st century, organizations have started to face the challenges of a complex, dynamic environment more harshly. Global competition, economic crises, changing technologies and market structures have put strong demands on organizations in terms of flexibility and innovation. In an uncertain and turbulent setting, organizations need to adopt highly flexible structures in order to survive. The flatter the organization is, the higher is the capability of the organization to cope with the requirements of the volatile, ambiguous environmental dynamics. In this respect, organizations have started to search for ways of facilitating creativity and innovation, and flatter organizational structures, decentralized decision-making processes and increased delegation have gained vital attention. As Hamel and Prahalad (2002) mention, hierarchies hinder initiation and creativity; therefore, it is impossible to empower subordinates under vertical organizational structures.

As stated by Deci and Ryan (1987), individuals have needs regarding self-determination and autonomy. With the help of decentralized and flat organizational structures, individuals are enabled to increase their autonomy, intrinsic motivation, and, through that, their performance. Intrinsic motivation is shown to have a positive impact on work outcomes such as creativity (e.g., Amabile, Hill, Hennessey, & Tighe, 1994; Shalley, Zhou, & Oldham, 2004); performance (e.g., Callahan, Brownlee, Brtek, & Tosi, 2003; Catley & Duda, 1997; Creasoli & Ford, 2014; Lin, McKeachie, & Kim, 2003; Vansteenkiste, Simons, Lens, Sheldon, & Deci, 2004; Wang & Guthrie, 2004); affective commitment (e.g., Ganesan & Weitz, 1996); and negative impact on turnover intentions (e.g., Houkes, Janssen, de Jonge, & Nijhuis, 2001; Richer, Blanchard, & Vallerand, 2002). Therefore, organizations that have horizontal structures and practices supporting decentralization can enhance the intrinsic motivation of employees which in return brings about strategic advantage for the organization itself.

This new orientation of organizations has led to new challenges regarding the expected leader behavior. The lateralization of organizational structures puts different demands on the management side, requiring a change in leadership style. When the evolution of leadership theories is considered, it can be seen that every theory has been developed as a response to the conditions and requirements of the day. For example, in the beginning of the 20th century, there was a strict control culture between the employers and employees via the effects of Scientific Management. Scientific Management mainly focused on the separation of workers and managers in terms of responsibility and was used as a way to ensure productivity through command and control chains. In this respect, it attributed the top-down control role to the leader. Whereas Scientific Management took place in the United States of America, different scholars in Europe held similar approaches towards leadership. Henri Fayol and Max Weber, differentiating in their contributions to management science, agreed on something; leadership was a top-down process (Pearce & Manz, 2005). All theories of leadership developed in this era coincided with this understanding. The Great-Man Theory, trait theories of leadership, they all determined a set of personality characteristics or sources of power which defined the role and success of the leader, leading to a romanticized conception of leadership (Meindl, Ehrlich, & Dukerich, 1985). The perfect outcome was dependent on the attributes of the leader and the leader could save or fail all.

Since the 1980s, new leadership approaches such as charismatic leadership and transformational leadership have grasped the attention of scholars. The idea behind these heroic leadership models was that the leader could inspire the followers, and, with the help of the vision created the organization could be able to survive in turbulent times. The problem with these heroic models of leadership was that it focused on just one side of the dyadic, reciprocal relationship between the leader and followers. It idealized and exaggerated the behavior of the leader and neglected the potential of the followers (Furtner & Baldegger, 2013). The highly creative and innovative employee behavior could not be achieved through the use of classical, established leadership approaches.

As an attempt to overcome this shortcoming, in 1990s and 2000s, post-heroic leadership models were introduced. The main difference of this approach was that it concentrated on both sides of the leader-follower relationship and emphasized the knowledge and development potential of the followers. Empowering leadership, shared leadership and self-leadership have emerged as the basic milestones of this approach. The behavior associated with these styles of leadership was the distribution of power and knowledge and procurement of more autonomy for the followers. The role of the leader turned into a mentoring function rather than a symbol of power. With the help of this post-heroic movement, the organizations have become more capable of enhancing the creativity and innovation required for them to survive in today's fluxional business environment.

In line with this, research has shown that, recently, organizations have displayed a tendency to increase autonomy (Wood, Stride, Wall, & Cleg, 2004). Contributing to the development of employees has helped to disseminate knowledge more easily, reduce response time and increase efficiency by cutting costs (Pearce & Manz, 2005). Participatory management activities and delegation have become vital for being flexible. In this respect, self-leadership offers potential for application in today's fluxional business world for organizations to survive and gain a competitive edge (Houghton & Yoho, 2005).

In the following section, the meaning and conceptualization of self-leadership is introduced and its dimensions are explained.

2.2 Self-leadership

As the studies over leadership increased, the importance of effective leadership and its outcomes have grasped the attention of scholars. Compared to other leadership theories, a more recent theory, "self-leadership", has been proposed to reevaluate the concept of leadership. First defined by Manz (1986), self-leadership is conceptualized as the process of motivating one's self in order to foster organizational and individual performance (Tabak, Sığrı, & Türkoz, 2013). The aim is to enable people to manage and control themselves. Hereby, the organization will be operating on a more lateral system that encourages autonomy and empowerment. It has its roots in "self-management" concept and is proposed as a "substitute for leadership" in this sense that self-leading individuals may not need to be supervised or controlled; they control and regulate themselves. It is a process whereby individuals direct and motivate themselves in order to perform the required tasks (Manz, 1986; Manz & Neck, 2004).

First coined by Kerr and Jermier (1978), "substitutes for leadership" theory asserts that situational factors may substitute for leadership. Some organizational factors such as job design or follower characteristics such as ability may replace the role of the leader and reinforce individual action. The main difference of the theory is that it recognizes the importance of the followers, demolishes the exaggerated role of the leader and explains why sometimes leaders fail. From a social learning theory perspective, Manz and Sims (1980) suggest that reinforcements such as environmental cues or rewards have an influence on employee behavior, and, if these reinforcements are not directed by the leader then they can be referred to as substitutes for leadership. In this respect, when an individual is capable of establishing self-reinforcement mechanisms, then this self-influence can also be regarded as a substitute for leadership. Therefore, self-management or self-leadership is also a substitute for leadership (Manz & Sims, 1980).

Effective leaders, first, have to lead themselves in order to be influential over others (Further & Baldegger, 2013). Therein, self-leadership is defined as a self-influencing process to increase personal effectiveness (Neck & Manz, 2010). More specifically, self-leadership is conceptualized as "a process through which individuals control their own behavior, influencing and leading themselves through the use of specific sets of behavioral and cognitive strategies" (Neck & Houghton, 2006, p. 270).

In literature, self-leadership strategies are classified under three headings: behavior-focused strategies, natural reward strategies and constructive thought pattern strategies (Manz & Neck, 2004; Manz & Sims, 2001; Prussia, Anderson, & Manz, 1998).

Behavior-focused strategies involve the self-regulation of behavior to increase self-awareness and to facilitate positive behaviors to complete necessary but unpleasant tasks and to suppress behaviors that may lead to failure (Houghton, Bonham, Neck, & Singh, 2004; Neck & Houghton, 2006). These strategies include self-observation, self-goal setting, self-cueing, self-reward and self-punishment (Manz & Neck, 2004). Self-observation includes increasing one's self-awareness in order to eliminate ineffective or unproductive behaviors and it helps to identify why and when an individual engages in certain kind of behaviors (Mahoney & Arnkoff, 1978, 1979; Manz & Neck, 2004; Manz & Sims, 1980). With the help of this information, one can define behavior-altering goals for himself/herself and this process is referred as self-goal setting (Manz, 1986; Manz & Neck, 2004; Manz & Sims, 1980). Self-set goals and self-set rewards enable individuals to put more effort into what they are doing and these kind of challenging goals are stated to have a positive effect on performance levels (Locke & Latham, 1990; Mahoney & Arnkoff, 1978, 1979; Manz & Neck, 2004; Manz & Sims, 1980). Self-rewards act as motivating mechanisms that help the individual to concentrate on an unpleasant task. Self-punishment refers to a self-correcting feedback that helps an individual to examine his/her failures and to reshape behaviors leading to this consequence. The last behavior-focused strategy, self-cueing refers to concrete, external mechanisms such as notes, posters etc. that help to encourage constructive behaviors and to reduce destructive ones while keeping attention on goal achievement (Manz & Neck, 2004; Manz & Sims, 1980, 2001).

Natural reward strategies help to seek out situations that enable the individual to be motivated by the inherently enjoyable facets of the task (Manz & Neck, 2004; Manz & Sims, 2001). These are comprised of two strategies: integrating more enjoyable features to a task or shifting attention from unpleasant features to pleasant features. These strategies both help to perceive the task as naturally rewarding (Manz & Neck, 2004; Manz & Sims, 2001). These strategies are also conceptualized as drivers of feelings of competence and self-determination which are associated with intrinsic motivation (Deci & Ryan, 1985).

The third group, constructive thought pattern strategies, refers to the creation and maintenance of habitual thinking patterns that aim to facilitate future performance (Houghton et al., 2004; Neck & Houghton, 2006). These strategies consist of identification and replacement of dysfunctional beliefs and assumptions, mental imagery and positive self-talk. Individuals should evaluate their own thought patterns to find out beliefs and assumptions hindering their future performance and negative self-talk should be eliminated, replacing it with positive, encouraging internal dialogues. What is meant by mental imagery is the envisioning of a successful future performance (Neck & Houghton, 2006). It is claimed that when individuals envision successful outcomes, it is more likely for them to achieve this pre-envisioned performance level when confronted with the actual task (Manz & Neck, 2004).

So far, research has mainly concentrated on the relationships between personality and self-leadership. As stated before, Houghton and colleagues (2004) have shown that self-leadership is correlated with extraversion and conscientiousness of the Big Five Personality Traits and Furtner and Rauthmann (2010) have found a relationship between self-leadership and traits of extraversion and openness to experience. As a part of the research between self-leadership and personality factors, the dark triad (narcissism, Machiavellianism, and psychopathy) was also investigated. It was found that narcissism had the strongest correlation with self-leadership (Furtner, Rauthmann, & Sachse, 2011).

To see the effect of self-leadership on job outcomes, many studies, both conceptually and empirically, explored the effect self-leadership on performance and showed that self-leadership had a positive impact on performance (e.g., Godwin, Neck, & Houghton, 1999; Neck & Manz, 1992; Prussia et al., 1998). As part of the research over other outcomes, self-leadership has been shown to contribute positively to career success (Murphy & Ensher, 2001), self-efficacy (Latham & Frayne, 1989; Prussia et al., 1998), and job satisfaction (Batt & Applebaum, 1995; Neck & Manz, 1996; Uhl-Bien & Graen, 1998).

Within the framework of this research, self-leadership is considered as both an antecedent and an outcome and the subject of interest is to find out some of the possible determinants and outcomes of this construct.

Chapter 3 Study 1 – Quantitative exploration of determinants and outcomes of self-leadership

Abstract: This chapter is based on the quantitative part of the research – Study 1. Study 1 includes the testing of two models that investigate some antecedents and outcomes of self-leadership. In this respect, first, the anticipated antecedents (transformational leadership, HPWS, proactive personality) and outcomes (work engagement, OCB) will be briefly defined. Afterwards, a theoretical explanation for the expected relationships will be provided. The effect of 1) transformational leadership, 2) high-performance work systems (HPWS), and 3) proactive personality on self-leadership will be discussed. Afterwards, the relationships between self-leadership and its impact on job outcomes 1) work engagement, and 2) organizational citizenship behavior (OCB) will be analyzed. The logic behind the expected relationships will be explained with regard to self-determination theory (SDT) (Ryan & Deci, 2000) on which the framework is rested upon. Accordingly, the hypotheses regarding these connections will be formulated and the research models will be presented. After that, the design of the research instruments, sampling procedure, data collection process and sample characteristics for Study 1 will be given. Reliability and validity of the measures will also be presented. Lastly, the hypothesized relationships will be tested.

3.1 Literature review

3.1.1 Transformational leadership

Over the past decade, there have been many leadership theories that have grasped the attention of researchers and practitioners. Some of these theories have emerged as cornerstones of leadership literature while others have vanished or lost significance over time. One of these highly established theories is the transformational leadership theory.

Transformational leadership, in line with what its name suggests, is concerned with activating a transformation within the organization. It involves altering minds, beliefs and values, illustrating and clarifying vision and purpose, and initiating change (Lewis, 1996).

Although it has been mistaken for charismatic leadership, the fact that transformational leadership is not solely concerned with personal transaction but rather with an idea of shared mission, charisma constitutes only a sub-dimension of transformational leadership (Bass, 1985). This mission is basically built upon the development of followers in a way that enables the transformation of followers to make them self-reliant and independent.

According to Avolio and Bass (1995), transformational leadership can be conceptualized under four dimensions or four leadership skills, namely, idealized influence, inspirational motivation, intellectual stimulation and individualized consideration.

Idealized Influence means that leaders become role models for the followers. The followers, in a way, idealize their leaders and feel trust, admiration and respect towards them increasing the leader's ability to influence and the followers' tolerance to accept change. Inspirational Motivation refers to what the leaders make to inspire followers to achieve both personal and organizational goals. The leader clearly communicates expectations that followers should meet and demonstrates commitment to goals and the shared vision (Avolio & Bass, 2002). Intellectual Stimulation refers to the stimulation of followers' efforts in order to make them more innovative and creative. Followers are encouraged to try new approaches and their ideas are not criticized if they differ from the leaders' ideas (Avolio & Bass, 2002). Individualized Consideration means treating followers as individuals and not just as members of a group (Dionne, Yammarino, Atwater, & Spangler, 2004). Leader supports and pays attentions to the needs of the followers while encouraging them to reach their full potential.

Within the scope of this research, a transformational leadership style is considered as a potential antecedent of increased self-leadership in followers.

3.1.2 High-performance work systems

As stated before, in current business environment, technological capabilities, innovation capacity and efficiency are not satisfactory to gain a competitive edge. The organizations' human resources play a crucial role to determine competitive advantage (Pfeffer, 1994) and the practices implemented by human resources departments have gained vital importance. Some organizations adopt HPWSs in order to achieve higher employee satisfaction and commitment.

High-performance work systems are considered as practices that are implemented to improve individuals' performance opportunities and motivations (Bozkurt, Ertemsir, & Bal, 2014). The aim is to stimulate employees' skills and efforts (Datta, Guthrie, & Wright, 2005). These systems are regarded as a way to promote employee commitment and autonomy by offering encouraging practices such as participation in decision making, training opportunities and information sharing (Lee & Bang, 2012). These practices are considered as a tool for improved performance and motivation, and, in return, as a way to competitive advantage (Becker & Huselid, 1998).

Scholars have identified different conceptualizations of HPWS. For example, according to Pfeffer (1998), HPWS consists of seven dimensions: employment security, selective hiring of new personnel, self-managed teams and decentralization of decision making, high compensation contingent on organizational performance, extensive training, reduced distinctions and barriers and extensive sharing of financial and performance information throughout the organization (Lee & Bang, 2012). The common themes or dimensions mentioned in previous research are selective staffing, extensive training, performance-contingent incentive compensation systems, benefits, commitment to employee development and flexible job assignments (e.g., Arthur, 1994; Datta et al., 2005; Guthrie, 2001; Huselid, 1995; Pfeffer, 1994; Wood & Wall, 2002). The consensus over these common themes implies that it is theoretically appropriate to accept HPWS as a single, generic construct (Becker & Huselid, 1998). The underlying principle of all conceptualizations is to enable employees control and manage themselves (Tomer, 2001).

According to Bamberger and Meshoulam (2000), strategic human resource management espoused two basic approaches to HPWS. The first one is the resource based view that sees the employees as resources and invests in the development of them via training and career opportunities, whereas the control approach is based on monitoring employee performance (Delery & Doty, 1996; Snell, 1992). Sun, Aryee and Law (2007) state that these high-performance work practices can be categorized under three headings: people flow, appraisal and rewards, and employment relation (p. 560). People flow includes staffing, mobility, job security and training. Sample practices are selective staffing, giving more extensive training, defining clear career paths and guarantying job security. Second dimension appraisal and rewards include practices such as long-term, results-oriented appraisal and extensive rewards. The last category, employment relation is based on the job characteristics. Clear job descriptions, flexible job assignments and participation are the basic practices that constitute this dimension.

Within the scope of this research, the conceptualization of Sun, Aryee and Law (2007) will be taken into account. According to their research, HPWS include eight sub-dimensions named as selective staffing, extensive training, internal mobility, employment security, clear job descriptions, results-oriented appraisal, incentive reward and participation. HPWS will be treated as a possible organizational determinant of self-leadership around these dimensions.

3.1.3 Proactive personality

Proactive personality has been defined as "the relatively stable tendency to effect environmental change" (Bateman & Crant, 1993, p. 103). Langer (1983) states that the proactive dimension of behavior is linked to the need by employees to manipulate and control their work settings. Proactive personality bears proactive behavior; according to Crant (1995), high proactive personality individuals are found to be able to identify opportunities, take action and persist until they bring about meaningful change (Frese & Fay, 2001).

Proactive personality is defined differently by different scholars. According to Crant (2000), proactive personality is "taking initiative in improving current circumstances or creating new ones; it involves challenging the status quo rather than passively adapting to present conditions" (p. 436). As other definitions propose, a person who is "relatively unconstrained by situational forces, and who effects environmental change" (Bateman & Crant, 1993, p. 105) and "whose behavior is characterized as self-directive and future focused, and who brings about change to the situation and/or change within himself or herself" (Bindle & Parker, 2010, p. 568) can be regarded as a proactive person.

A person who has a proactive personality is likely to exert proactive behaviors more often. In this respect, some common behaviors exhibited by proactive people can be identified. According to Dubrin (2013), the characteristics of a proactive worker can be listed as desire for control, taking charge at work, having high cognitive skills and high self-efficacy, setting challenging goals, seeking for opportunities, judging independently and speaking out, and assessing the probable success of the proactive behavior.

Proactive personality is treated as a distinct concept that is not covered in the Big Five Personality Model (Goldberg, 1990). The five traits, namely Neuroticism, Extraversion, Agreeableness, Openness and Conscientiousness are regarded as the milestones of personality (McCrae & John, 1992). Although seen distinct, research has shown that proactive personality is correlated with extraversion and conscientiousness besides need for achievement and need for dominance (Crant & Bateman, 1993). In this respect, Crant and Bateman (2000) state that proactive personality is able to represent "some unique elements of personality not accounted for by the five-factor model" (p. 66).

Proactive personality is also found to be positively and significantly related to participation in organizational improvement initiatives (Parker, 1998), entrepreneurial behavior (Becherer & Maurer, 1999), effective leadership (Bateman & Crant, 1993; Crant & Bateman, 2000), innovation (Kickul & Guidry, 2002), employee performance and work team performance (Crant, 1995).

Proactive personality is considered as another possible determinant which is expected to serve as an example to explain the dispositional side of self-leadership.

3.1.4 Work engagement

With the rise of the positive psychology movement, concepts such as work commitment, work engagement, organizational citizenship behavior and job involvement have gained the attention of practitioners and academics. In today's challenging work environment, it is not enough to wipe off the demotivating factors in work setting, but it is also required to present an added-value for employees in order to sustain their high-performance and attachment. Employees do not solely need to be granted survival at work, but they also need to actualize themselves and go beyond their minimum level of satisfaction in order to feel that their job is meaningful to them.

Emerging from that point of view, work engagement has gained attention in recent years and is derived from the concept of "personal engagement" first coined by Kahn (1990). In his research, Kahn tried to identify the situations in which employees feel engaged to and feel alienated from their jobs. To define, Kahn (1990) refers to engagement as "harnessing of organizational members' selves to their work roles" and states that "in engagement people employ and express themselves physically, cognitively and emotionally during role performances" (p. 694). An individual keeps himself/herself psychically, cognitively and emotionally busy in terms of work and an individual can be defined as engaged in his/her work if he/she participates physically in work roles, feels cognitively vigilant and emotionally involved in job (Kahn, 1990, pp. 694–700).

Although lacking operationalization, Kahn's definition has established the baseline for defining engagement. After Kahn, Maslach and Leiter (1997) came up with a more measurable definition and claimed engagement to be "the opposite of burnout". According to this conceptualization, engagement and burnout were characterized as two opposite sides of a continuum on which an individual stands at any time.

Exhaustion, cynicism and lack of professional efficacy are determinants of burnout that is defined as a psychological syndrome (Leiter & Maslach, 2004). On the other hand, engagement is intertwined with high levels of energy, interest in job and feelings of competence. Therefore, Maslach, Jackson and Leiter (1996) proposed these two concepts to be opposites and claimed that it was possible to measure the level of engagement through the use of burnout scales. Schaufeli, Salanova, Gonzalez-Roma and Bakker (2002) objected to that definition. Their assertion was that these two concepts could not be opposites; they were totally different. According to their conceptualization, engagement was "a positive, fulfilling, work-related state of mind that is characterized by vigor, dedication and absorption" (Schaufeli et al., 2002, pp. 464–481). Without doubt, this definition has also aroused counter arguments and has been challenged over the years; but this conceptualization is the one widely accepted and respected in relevant literature. In this conceptualization, engagement is considered to be a three-dimensional construct. These dimensions are vigor, dedication and absorption. Vigor refers to the high levels of energy and mental resilience at work; dedication refers to the pride and enthusiasm felt during work, and absorption refers to the concentration in work. These three dimensions imply that the individual cannot be detached from work and is persistent in doing his/her job in a way that the work inspires and challenges him/her (Schaufeli & Bakker, 2003, p. 5).

Engagement can be facilitated through different mechanisms. In literature, the determinants or antecedents of engagement that help to understand how it can be triggered or augmented are widely examined. At individual, team or organizational level, there are many factors that can contribute to the variance in work engagement. Control, autonomy and empowerment are seen as some of the vital antecedents of engagement. It has been stated that engagement is positively correlated with intrinsic motivation (Chalofsky & Krishna, 2009). Ryan and Deci (2000) emphasize that individuals' basic needs lead them to be intrinsically motivated to reach their goals and the positive emotions brought about by this process contributes to engagement (Park, Song, & Lim, 2016). In addition to that, some organizational factors such as fair compensation, feedback, support of peers and superiors, job variety and training opportunities are found to be positively related to work engagement (Demerouti, Bakker, Nachreiner, & Schaufeli, 2001; Leiter & Maslach, 1988).

According to Roberts and O'Davenport (2002), factors contributing to work engagement can be classified under three categories: career development, organizational identification and rewarding of the work. According to career development, when the employee senses that he/she has an opportunity to climb up the hierarchy or to get promoted, he/she will be more engaged to his/her work. Organizational identification, on the other hand, refers to the propensity of an employee to identify with and to feel as a part of the organization. These sorts of factors are also considered as facilitators of work engagement. Lastly, the rewarding of the work refers to the compensation of an individual in return for his/her efforts. When the individual believes that he/she is fairly treated, then his/her level of engagement is expected to increase (Trahant, 2007).

Work engagement is considered as a possible outcome of self-leadership and, therefore, is expected to increase as self-leadership skills of employees increase.

3.1.5 Organizational citizenship behavior

Organizational citizenship behavior (OCB) is defined as "individual behavior that is discretionary, not directly or explicitly recognized by the formal reward system, and that in the aggregate promotes the effective functioning of the organization" (Organ, 1988). As indicated by the definition, this refers to an altruistic behavior that is not rewarded by the organization and is not included in the formal job description (İşbaşı, 2000).

The most widely accepted and used conceptualization of OCB is developed by Organ (1988). The factors constituting OCB are altruism, courtesy, sportsmanship, conscientiousness and civic virtue. Altruism refers to the voluntary actions carried out to help another person. Civic virtue is related to involvement in the political process of organization such as expressing opinions and attending meetings. Conscientiousness is about going over the minimum role requirements; it means to attend more than required, to be punctual or to conserve resources. Sportsmanship is the employee's acceptance of organization related circumstances without complaining and courtesy refers to the altruistic behaviors that are done in order to prevent conflicts within the workplace.

Within the scope of this study, another conceptualization will be used. A more recent categorization of OCB is done by Williams and Anderson (1991). In this study, the researchers differentiate between organizational citizenship behaviors towards individuals and towards organization, referring to them respectively as OCBI and OCBO. OCBO is related to the behaviors of the individual that benefit the organization or prevent harm towards the organization, such as reporting when unable to come to work. OCBI is related with the activities which are targeted towards individuals within the workplace but also which indirectly benefit the organization, such as helping colleagues altruistically (Willams & Anderson, 1991).

When the motives behind engaging in OCB are investigated, it is seen that impression management, prosocial values and organizational concerns are effective (Rioux & Penner, 2001). These different motives defined whether the individual engaged in OCBI or OCBO. People who were concerned about their careers and future were more likely to engage in OCBI, because helping behaviors directed towards individuals can be more visible compared to behaviors directed towards organization. It is based on the expectation that one will see and appreciate the altruistic efforts.

The second type of motive which is based on prosocial values is rooted in the basic premise of the concept; people really want to be helpful to others. In this respect, individuals holding prosocial values are more likely to engage in OCBI as they really care for the well-being of others (Rioux & Penner, 2001).

The last motive mentioned by Rioux and Penner is organizational concerns. This motive is associated with social exchange theory. It is asserted that people want to reciprocate for the opportunities the organization has offered them. In this respect, this motive leads people to engage in OCBO (Rioux & Penner, 2001). Finkelstein (2011) made another distinction between these motives and stated that organizational concerns and prosocial values correspond with intrinsic motivational orientation, whereas impression management is a more self-serving motive. Therefore, impression management is more related to extrinsic motivation. The study concluded that all these motives worked together to help the individual reach his/her goals and people consciously performed OCB in order to satisfy different motives (Finkelstein, 2011).

Within the scope of this research, OCBI and OCBO are considered as possible outcomes of performing self-leadership strategies.

3.1.6 Self-efficacy

Self-efficacy has been defined as "the extent to which an individual believes him or herself capable of successfully performing a specific behavior" (Prussia et al., 1998). It is the belief a person holds about his/her capabilities to produce pre-determined levels of performance. Self-efficacy beliefs affect the feelings, thoughts, motivations and behaviors of individuals through cognitive, affective, motivational and selection processes (Bandura, 1994).

Individuals high on self-efficacy beliefs tend to be more confident in mastering challenging tasks and they are not inclined to avoid these kind of obstacles (Bandura, 1994; Prussia et al., 1998). Research in different fields has demonstrated examples that self-efficacy was positively influenced by self-management techniques (e.g., Dilorio, Faherty, & Manteuffel, 1992; Frayne & Latham, 1987). Prussia and colleagues (1998) also showed that self-efficacy mediated the relationship between self-leadership and performance outcomes. In this respect, within the framework of this study, self-efficacy is expected to mediate the relationships between self-leadership and job outcomes.

3.2 Conceptual framework and hypotheses development

3.2.1 Theoretical framework

Within the framework of this research, SDT is used as the base on which the anticipated relationships are grounded. Self-determination is regarded as "the capacity to choose and to have those choices, rather than reinforcement contingencies, drives, or any other forces or pressures, be the determinants of one's actions" (Deci & Ryan, 1985, p. 38). Besides being a capacity, self-determination is also considered as a need and, in this respect, this theory is an approach where individuals' innate psychological needs that form the basis for their motivation and personality integration are taken into account (Ryan & Deci, 2000).

People are by nature inclined to be self-determining. With the help of this predisposition, one can adapt himself to the environment or change the environment according to himself/herself. The hallmark of this theory is based on the assumption that people have the flexibility to choose; when self-determined, one will act out of choice rather than obligation or cohesion. In this respect, one can control his/her environment or can decide not to control. SDT is not stated to be fully independent from the environment. It asserts that the opportunity to be self-determining can be affected by environmental forces, which can either support or hinder the level of self-determination.

According to SDT, there are three basic needs that should be met in order to facilitate the necessary conditions for growth, integration, social development and well-being. These needs are competence, relatedness and autonomy. Competence refers to the apprehension of requirements to reach pre-determined internal/external outcomes and of how to be effective in performing these actions. Relatedness means establishing satisfying, secure relationships with others in a social network and autonomy refers to the opportunity of being able to regulate and direct one's own actions. The concept of needs is essential to define the conditions that facilitate motivation, performance and development. If an environment offers opportunities to satisfy these needs, then motivation, performance and development are expected to be at their maximum level (Deci, Vallerand, Pelletier, & Ryan, 1991).

SDT claims that people are inherently inclined to learn and develop. When this inherent inclination occurs in the absence of external rewards, then it is called intrinsic motivation. Intrinsic motivation is stated as engaging in an activity "for its own sake" (Ryan & Deci, 2000).

As cognitive evaluation theory (a sub-theory of SDT) suggests, satisfying competence and autonomy needs are essential to maintain and enhance intrinsic motivation, and, therefore, conditions that help to develop feelings of competence and autonomy are expected to increase intrinsic motivation. Also, it is stated that, satisfaction of the need for relatedness is important to enable intrinsic motivational processes to occur, because when people feel rejected by the environment it is harder for them to experience pleasure and enjoyment in the activities they carry on. (Ryan & Deci, 2007)

The two other main motivation types included within self-determination theory are extrinsic motivation and amotivation. Extrinsic motivation refers to being motivated by expected outcomes that the activity does not inherently offer, whereas amotivation refers to having no enthusiasm toward the completion of an action.

Extrinsic motivation sources differ with respect to their autonomy levels. It means that some of these external forces may be volitional whereas the others may be compelling to the self. This mini-theory is coined with the name organismic integration theory by Deci and Ryan (1985). Within this respect, they have proposed a model that illustrates the relativity and causality of the basic tenets of the theory (Figure 1). As seen from the figure, the environmental contingencies determine the kind of motivation that shapes the respective behavior. Another factor in organismic integration theory, perceived locus of control, refers to the motivation being autonomous or controlled from the outside. It helps to understand how a contingency is internalized, meaning that higher autonomy enables the contingencies to be integrated due to the fact that they serve internal goals rather than external ones (Ryan & Deci, 2007).

Figure 1: Schematic representation of self-determination theory illustrating the features of three of the component subtheories: basic psychological needs theory, cognitive evaluation theory, and organismic integration theory (Ryan & Deci, 2007, p. 8 in ed. Hagger & Chatzisarantis, 2007).

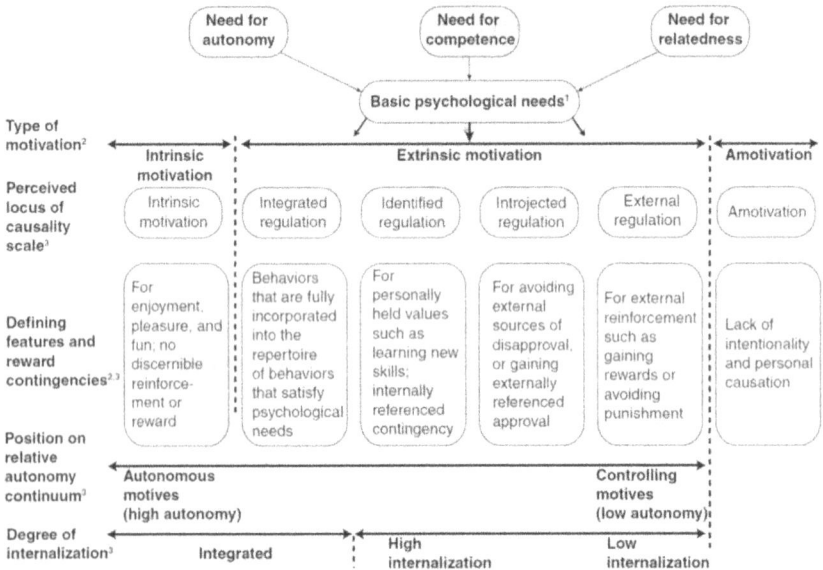

Need for autonomy   Need for competence   Need for relatedness

Basic psychological needs[1]

Type of motivation[2]	Intrinsic motivation	Extrinsic motivation				Amotivation
Perceived locus of causality scale[3]	Intrinsic motivation	Integrated regulation	Identified regulation	Introjected regulation	External regulation	Amotivation
Defining features and reward contingencies[2,3]	For enjoyment, pleasure, and fun; no discernible reinforcement or reward	Behaviors that are fully incorporated into the repertoire of behaviors that satisfy psychological needs	For personally held values such as learning new skills; internally referenced contingency	For avoiding external sources of disapproval or gaining externally referenced approval	For external reinforcement such as gaining rewards or avoiding punishment	Lack of intentionality and personal causation
Position on relative autonomy continuum[3]	Autonomous motives (high autonomy)			Controlling motives (low autonomy)		
Degree of internalization[3]	Integrated		High internalization	Low internalization		

28

In this respect, SDT is taken as the overarching theory to explain the anticipated relationships within the framework of this research.

3.2.2 Hypotheses development

Leadership research has shown that the relationships employees establish with their leaders are critical in understanding the mechanisms that lead the employees to reach their full potential and become self-motivated. Manz and Sims (1987) have shown that some leader behaviors that encourage mechanisms such as self-criticism and self-goal setting are required for employees to develop self-leadership skills. Accordingly, we state that understanding the drivers of self-leadership is essential in order to offer the employees the necessary conditions that would enable them to utilize their potential. In this respect, we propose two models that integrate the possible drivers of self-leadership skills and combine it with expected outcomes in order to see its vitality for organization.

3.2.2.1 Determinants of self-leadership

Self-leadership is considered as an important factor that affects the enthusiasm, commitment and performance of employees especially in empowering organizations (Manz, 1986, 1990). Also, in a training intervention based study by Neck and Manz (1996) it was seen that self-leadership training led to increased performance, positive affect, job satisfaction and decreased negative affect.

Before we examine possible dispositional factors that foster self-leadership, we have decided to understand if interventions to the context may have an effect on self-leadership skills to be triggered. As stated before, leadership styles encouraging employee participation such as transformational leadership are considered as necessary tools in facilitating self-leadership (Stewart et al., 2011). As Avolio and Gibbons (1988) suggest, transformational leadership first aims to encourage self-management. Therefore, we hypothesize that a leader who has pledged himself/herself to the development of the followers and who aims creating new leaders may be one of the drivers of this phenomenon. Transformational leaders are stated to nourish followers' abilities to think independently and creatively (Bass & Avolio, 1990). Studies showing the positive contribution of transformational leadership on empowerment also provide support for the anticipated relationship between transformational leadership and self-leadership (e.g., Dvir, Eden, Avolio, & Shamir, 2002; Jung, Chow, & Wu, 2003). In this respect, we propose transformational leadership as a possible determinant of self-leadership.

Transformational leaders do not rely on supervision and strict control; they rather develop others to learn self-regulation. From a self-determination perspective, the characteristics of a transformational leader that emphasize the use of listening, creating a vision, developing people etc. can be considered as satisfying the basic psychological needs of an individual. With the help of the transformational leader, people may feel more competent, more autonomous and related to a community. In this respect, the developmental opportunities and support offered by the leader help the individual to be intrinsically motivated towards a task and to feel that he/she has control over the work. Gagne and Deci (2005) state that satisfying the three psychological needs is essential while it leads to intrinsic motivation by increasing the enjoyment and challenge of the work itself. When an individual feels free to decide, challenged to learn new skills, and cared by others, then his/her psychological needs for autonomy, competence and relatedness will be satisfied respectively. Accordingly, the following hypothesis is formulated:

Hypothesis 1:   There will be a positive relationship between transformational leadership and self-leadership. As transformational leadership characteristics of supervisors increase, their employees will tend to exhibit higher levels of self-leadership skills.

Very similar to this rationale, we propose that another driver of self-leadership may be HPWSs. Self-leadership research has been intertwined with individual level drivers of self-leadership, but at the organizational level the research is limited to training and reward systems. Training and the structure of reward systems have been shown to affect the use of self-leadership strategies (Stewart et al., 2011). In this respect, this research aims to provide a more general framework that integrates training, reward systems, job descriptions, participation, mobility etc. and proposes HPWSs as a possible facilitator of self-leadership at the organizational level.

    Tomer (2001) states that in HPWSs, employees do not need to be controlled because what HPWSs try to create is an environment based on employee participation, commitment and empowerment. These systems are intended to increase the skills and knowledge of the employees and their willingness to exert effort (Bozkurt, Ertemsir, & Bal, 2014). As self-leadership does, HPWSs also emphasize the control and regulation of behavior by the employee. It aims to inspire employees to put more effort and to work harder. From a self-determination perspective, the practices carried out by the HR department and the organization will help the individual to satisfy his/her psychological needs of competence, autonomy and relatedness. In this respect, the training opportunities, implications of job security, empowerment practices etc. are expected to lead the individual to be motivated towards a task. Even if the task is not inherently enjoyable and rewarding, Ryan and Deci (2007) state that for personally held values such as learning new skills, an employee may internalize the extrinsic reward offered by the activity and this contingency may help him/her to satisfy his/her basic psychological needs. An individual is expected to regulate his/her cognitions or behaviors to achieve that given goal, and, therefore, HPWS are expected to contribute to self-leadership positively.

Hypothesis 2:   There will be a positive relationship between high-performance work systems and self-leadership. As employees perceive high-performance work systems to be carried out more, they will tend to exhibit higher levels of self-leadership skills.

In terms of dispositional factors, all studies have been conducted around Big Five Personality Traits. For example, Stewart et al. (1996) have shown that individuals high in conscientiousness engage in self-leadership compared to individuals low in conscientiousness. This area still lacks research about different personality traits' effects on self-leadership. Therefore, it is claimed that, proactive personality can be a determinant of self-leadership skills. Proactive personality and self-leadership operate according to the same rationale – controlling the external environment – and some researchers have claimed self-management to be a proactive behavior (Saks & Ashforth, 1997). Proactive people are likely to believe that they can change their destinies with the help of the potential they believe they have and consequently become successful. Self-leadership strategies such as self-regulation, self-goal-setting etc. require active efforts to manage and modify behavior to reach success; therefore, proactive people are more likely to have these characteristics and use self-leadership strategies (Gerhardt, Ashenbaum, & Newman, 2009). People who exhibit proactive personality characteristics are eager to change the environment, open to innovation and striving for control. In this respect, it is expected that, individuals who have proactive personality will be more likely to exert self-leadership skills.

As stated before, SDT is based on the assumption that people are free to choose for themselves. Proactive personality and self-leadership, in this respect, coincide with the premises of SDT. Proactive people can control the environment and act according to their will. In this respect, they do not require an external force to take action. Intrinsically motivated, they move towards their goals as self-leaders do. Based on this rationale, the following hypothesis is introduced.

Hypothesis 3:   There will be a positive relationship between proactive personality and self-leadership. The more proactive a person is the higher levels of self-leadership skills he/she will exhibit.

3.2.2.2 Outcomes of self-leadership

As outcomes of self-leadership, we have introduced work engagement and organizational citizenship behavior. We propose that self-leadership is an important predictor of these job outcomes.

Previous research has shown that individuals who use self-leadership strategies tend to "develop a sense of ownership over their tasks and work processes" which, in turn, may lead to higher levels of commitment (Neck & Houghton, 2006).

Reviewing self-leadership literature, Stewart et al. (2011) summarized individual and team level outcomes of self-leadership. In this review, it is seen that many studies revealed positive relationships between self-leadership and work outcomes. For example, Birdi et al. (2008) found that increasing self-control led to increased employee productivity whereas Saks and Ashforth (1997) showed that greater internal control resulted in decreased stress and anxiety. Rise in levels of self-efficacy is considered as another major outcome of self-leadership (Latham & Frayne, 1989; Prussia et al., 1998). Higher levels of job satisfaction and innovative behavior and lower levels of absenteeism are also found to be in relation with increased self-leadership (Carmeli, Meitar, & Weisberg, 2006; Frayne & Latham, 1987; Latham & Frayne, 1989; Neck & Manz, 1996; Uhl-Bien & Graen, 1998). In addition, a study conducted by Park, Yun, and Han (2009) showed that self-leadership positively contributed to organizational citizenship behavior.

Neck and Manz (1996) have shown that there is a positive relationship between self-leadership training and positive affect and job satisfaction. Self-leadership is also claimed to enhance perceptions of meaningfulness, purpose and competence through empowerment (Lee & Koh, 2001). Neck and Houghton (2006) suggest that use of self-leadership strategies can affect variables such as commitment, trust, job satisfaction and improved performance, increasing the likelihood that they will occur.

In line with this proposition, we suggest that self-leadership skills may predict work behaviors in a way that as employees learn to use self-leadership skills they will be more engaged in their work and they will be inclined to show more altruistic behaviors. From a self-determination perspective, self-leadership strategies require an intrinsic motivation to regulate behavior. As we have conceptualized before, self-leadership skills can be enhanced through the satisfaction of different psychological needs. In this respect, this satisfaction and inner motivation are expected to lead to positive work outcomes such as engagement and OCB. When the basic three needs of an individual are satisfied, intrinsic motivation will be enhanced and this will lead to the internalization of extrinsic motivation.

This process will result in significant job outcomes such as behavior change, effective performance, increased job satisfaction, positive job attitudes, organizational citizenship behaviors and well-being (Gagne & Deci, 2005, p. 337). Other studies have shown that autonomous motivation is correlated with prosocial behavior and is likely to bear organizational citizenship behaviors (Penner, Midili, & Kegelmeyer, 1997). Also, the satisfaction of these basic three needs have been shown to positively contribute to work engagement (Deci et al., 2001). In this respect, it is expected that self-leaders who are able to satisfy these basic needs will be more likely to engage in positive job behaviors.

Hypothesis 4:   There will be a positive relationship between self-leadership and work engagement. As employees exhibit more self-leadership skills, they are expected to be more engaged to work.

As mentioned before, individuals engage in OCB due to different motives or different motivational orientations. Finkelstein (2011) showed that intrinsic motives such as prosocial values predicted OCBO whereas OCBI was affected from both intrinsic and extrinsic motives. Although stemming from different sources, a self-leader is expected to perform organizational citizenship behaviors. A person with high self-leadership skills may engage in OCBI in order to show his/her capabilities and to make his/her improvement visible. Another individual may engage in OCBO in order to reciprocate for the development opportunities offered by the organization. In this respect, OCBI and OCBO are expected to display a positive relationship with self-leadership.

Hypothesis 5a: There will be a positive relationship between self-leadership and organizational citizenship behavior towards other individuals (OCBI). As employees exhibit more self-leadership skills, their organizational citizenship behavior towards individuals are expected to increase.

Hypothesis 5b: There will be a positive relationship between self-leadership and organizational citizenship behavior towards the organization (OCBO). As employees exhibit more self-leadership skills, their organizational citizenship behavior towards organization is expected to increase.

3.2.2.3 Mediating role of self-efficacy

Norris (2008) showed that there is a positive relationship between general self-efficacy and self-leadership. It is stated that self-efficacy is a motivational belief and it affects how people behave in a variety of situations (Chen, Gully, &

Eden, 2004). Therefore, it has a motivational part and can be enhanced through the use of self-leadership strategies. Self-efficacy is "the belief in one's capabilities to organize and execute the courses of action required to produce given attainments" (Bandura, 1997, p. 3). Self-leadership, therefore, is a tool to increase self-efficacy because it enhances one's belief in self, capacity to organize and motivation to achieve an aim. Therefore, in line with self-determination theory, we propose that self-efficacy may play a mediator role between self-leadership and anticipated outcomes which are performance, OCB and work engagement.

A wide range of authors mention that the primary goal of self-leadership is to increase one's self-efficacy in order to get higher performance (e.g., Manz, 1986; Manz & Neck, 1999; Neck & Manz, 1992). It has been stated that higher levels of self-efficacy are correlated with increased effort to pursue a goal (Bandura & Cervone, 1983). Self-efficacy identifies what kind of behaviors a person will engage in, how persistent they will be, and how much effort they will spend to succeed (Satterfield & Davidson, 2000). People who have a tendency to overcome difficulties through self-initiated change and who are more goal-oriented, are generally high on self-efficacy levels (Maddux, 2002). In this respect, self-efficacy is claimed to be "the primary mechanism through which self-leadership affects performance" (Neck & Houghton, 2006, p. 29).

Prussia and colleagues (1998), and after that, Konradt, Andressen and Ellwart (2009) showed empirically that self-efficacy mediates the relationship between self-leadership and performance in different settings. As self-determination theory suggests, the use of self-leadership strategies enhances one's belief in controlling the environment and reaching the pre-determined goal. In this respect, we hypothesize that self-leadership will contribute to self-efficacy positively.

Hypothesis 6:   There will be a positive relationship between self-leadership and self-efficacy. People who exhibit higher levels of self-leadership skills, are likely to have higher levels of self-efficacy.

In a parallel fashion, self-efficacy is expected to mediate the relationship between self-leadership and work engagement. Self-leadership provides individuals with psychological resources that enrich their positive affect resources (Unsworth & Mason, 2012) which means that they are enabled to exert positive job attitudes when they feel that they have the control. According to SDT, individuals are motivated by their need for growth and self-regulation which lead them towards goal-oriented behavior (Deci & Ryan, 1985). Self-leadership helps them to feel autonomous and more confident resulting in higher levels of self-efficacy. This internal strength or resource, in turn, serves as the catalyzer for engaging in work (Bakker & Leiter, 2010; Xanthopoulou, Bakker, Demerouti, & Schaufeli, 2007).

Feelings of autonomy and competence, therefore, increase one's willingness to exert effort for their job.

Hypothesis 7: Self-efficacy will mediate the relationship between self-leadership and work engagement.

As stated before, self-leadership strategies require an intrinsic motivation to regulate behavior. With this in mind, self-efficacy levels of individuals are expected to increase. As mentioned above, self-efficacy helps to be more goal-oriented and to exert more effort. In this respect, individuals are likely to exert effort more than required. This means that, self-leadership may enhance altruistic behaviors such as organizational citizenship behavior through increased levels of self-efficacy. Motowidlo, Borman and Schmit (1997) have stated that OCB is affected by an individual's self-efficacy level. In line with that, Beauregard (2012) showed that self-efficacy contributed positively to OCB for men who were stated to be more achievement oriented. In this respect, it is expected that self-efficacy will act as a mediator in the relationship between self-leadership and OCBs.

Hypothesis 8a: Self-efficacy will mediate the relationship between self-leadership and OCBI.

Hypothesis 8b: Self-efficacy will mediate the relationship between self-leadership and OCBO.

The list of the hypotheses can be found in Table 1.

Table 1: List of Hypotheses

No.	Hypothesis
H1:	There will be a positive relationship between transformational leadership and self-leadership. As transformational leadership characteristics of supervisors increase, their employees will tend to exhibit higher levels of self-leadership skills.
H2:	There will be a positive relationship between high-performance work systems and self-leadership. As employees perceive high-performance work systems to be carried out more, they will tend to exhibit higher levels of self-leadership skills.
H3:	There will be a positive relationship between proactive personality and self leadership. The more proactive a person is, the higher levels of self-leadership skills he/she is expected to exhibit.
H4:	There will be a positive relationship between self-leadership and work engagement. As employees exhibit more self-leadership skills, they are expected to be more engaged in work.

No.	Hypothesis
H5a:	There will be a positive relationship between self-leadership and OCBI. As employees exhibit more self-leadership skills, their organizational citizenship behavior towards individuals are expected to increase.
5b:	There will be a positive relationship between self-leadership and OCBO. As employees exhibit more self-leadership skills, their organizational citizenship behavior towards organization are expected to increase.
H6:	There will be a positive relationship between self-leadership and self-efficacy. People who exhibit higher levels of self-leadership skills, are likely to have higher levels of self-efficacy.
H7:	Self-efficacy will mediate the relationship between self-leadership and work engagement.
H8a:	Self-efficacy will mediate the relationship between self-leadership and OCBI.
H8b:	Self-efficacy will mediate the relationship between self-leadership and OCBI.

The proposed models regarding the hypotheses are given in Figure 2 and Figure 3.

Figure 2: Proposed model 1

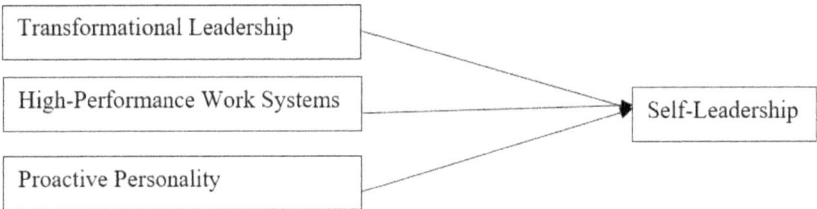

Figure 3: Proposed model 2

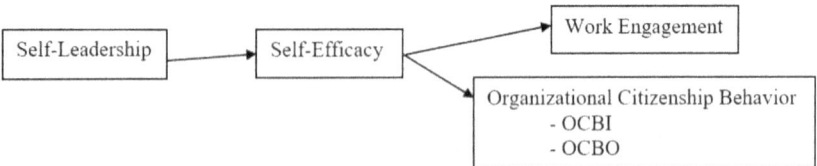

3.3 Research design and methodology

In this section, the research design and methodology of Study 1 will be discussed. The research consists of two separate studies. The first study was conducted by survey method. It includes two models regarding different research questions. The second study was conducted via semi-structured in-depth interviews.

This part explains the design of the research instruments, sampling procedure, data collection and sample characteristics for Study 1. Reliability and validity of the measures are also presented.

3.3.1 Sampling and data collection

With regard to the characteristics of the models, the research was conducted in firms operating mainly in services sector. To be more specific, we have collected our questionnaires mainly from the tourism, banking, insurance and food and beverages sector, and from firms having minimum 50 employees. In order for the number of respondents to be above the statistical significance threshold, we had aimed to collect a minimum number of 200 questionnaires and we have reached the number of 258 respondents.

Data for variables except OCB were collected from the employee, and OCB data were collected from the supervisors in order to prevent single-source bias. The demographics part was added to the questionnaires as the results could demonstrate significant differences according to demographic categories. In this respect, the questionnaires were sent to a professional research company and the firms who meet the research criteria were identified. The research company contacted these firms and data collection process took start. Representatives from the research company went to the firms and explained the aim of the research briefly. The questionnaires were transformed into an online-survey and the study was conducted over tablet computers in order to save time and paper. All questions were answered at a time. The data collection lasted a month and 258 usable questionnaires from the employees and 258 usable questionnaires from the supervisors were collected. After the process was complete, the final raw data was sent to us.

3.3.2 Sample characteristics

Two hundred and fifty eight participants and forty six supervisors took part in the study. One hundred and sixty four (63.5%) of the respondents are male whereas ninety four (36.5%) are female. The age of the participants differ from 18 to 62 with an average of 28.6. The tenure in work life ranges from 1 year to 40 years with an average of 8.2 years. Tenure in current organization is minimum 1 year and maximum 20 years and the mean is 3.6 years. Forty two (16.3%) of the participants have secondary school degree, one hundred and sixty (62%) have high school degree, fifty four (20.9%) have university degree and two (0.8%) have Masters or PhD degree.

The employees work in different branches ranging from food and beverage to customer services but all the organizations operate in service industry. One hundred and thirty eight (53.5%) of the participants work in retail sector (sales); sixty one (23.6%) in customer services (after sales); forty nine (19%) in food and beverage; and ten (3.9%) in financial services.

The sample demographics can be found in Table 2 on the next page.

Table 2: Sample Demographics of Study 1

Characteristic	Category	Frequency	Percent
Gender	Men	164	63.5%
	Women	94	36.5%
Age	Younger than 25	101	39.1%
	26–35	120	46.5%
	36–45	30	11.6%
	46–55	5	1.9%
	Older than 56	2	0.8%
Tenure in Work Life	Up to 5 years	119	46.1%
	6–10 years	73	28.3%
	11–15 years	38	14.7%
	More than 15 years	28	10.9%
Tenure in Current Organization	Up to 5 years	205	79.5%
	6–10 years	41	15.9%
	11–15 years	10	3.9%
	More than 15 years	2	0.8%
Education Level	Secondary School	42	16.3%
	High School	160	62%
	University	54	20.9%
	Masters or PhD	2	0.8%
Sector	Retail	138	53.5%
	Customer Services	61	23.6%
	Food and Beverage	49	19%
	Financial Services	10	3.9%

3.3.3 Measures

In this section the instruments used for the utilization of the constructs are presented and item purification is conducted through exploratory factor analyses.

Study 1 consists of two research models. The first model aims to test the influence of transformational leadership, high-performance work systems and proactive personality on self-leadership. Transformational leadership and high-performance work systems are introduced as possible contextual determinants of self-leadership whereas proactive personality is included as a dispositional antecedent. On the other hand, the second model is concerned with the outcomes. Work engagement and organizational citizenship behavior are included as anticipated outcomes of self-leadership. Self-leadership is expected to contribute positively to work engagement and organizational citizenship behavior. Lastly, self-efficacy is conceptualized as a possible mediator in the relationships between self-leadership and anticipated outcomes. In this respect, all the constructs and the respective tools used for measurement are presented together in this section.

First, in order to measure transformational leadership construct, the relevant items of the Multifactor Leadership Questionnaire (MLQ) developed by Bass and Avolio (1995) is distributed to the participants to rate their actual leader. MLQ is considered as the benchmark measure of transformational leadership. It involves 20 items related to four sub-dimensions of transformational leadership. Items are rated on a 5-point Likert scale ranging from 1 (definitely disagree) to 5 (definitely agree). Exploratory factor analysis (EFA) revealed a 1-factor structure for transformational leadership and all items loaded under 1 factor. Despite the different natures of the four components, it has been seen that the scale sometimes fails in terms of construct validity (e.g., Bycio, Hackett, & Allen, 1995). Bycio et al. (1995) reported that the correlation among the dimensions were high and did not yield distinguishing relationships with outcome variables. In this respect, the 1-factor structure can be considered as a possible phenomenon. In terms of item loadings, each item revealed a loading greater than 0.5; therefore, all items were kept for further analyses. Cronbach's Alpha score was found to be 0.981 and it demonstrated a very high score for reliability.

HPWSs were measured with the scale developed by Sun, Aryee and Law (2007). 22 items of the questionnaire were used. It consists of eight dimensions: selective staffing, extensive training, internal mobility, employment security, clear job descriptions, incentive reward and participation. The items were rated on a 5-point scale ranging from 1 (definitely disagree) to 5 (definitely agree). Exploratory factor analysis (EFA) revealed a 1-factor structure for HPWS similar to the results for transformational leadership. In literature, it has been stated that although particular dimensions or specific human resource practices may affect individuals differently, it cannot be understood whether this is the result of a single dimension or the HPWS as a whole based on the design of the study (e.g., Lee, Werner, & Kim, 2016; Takeuchi, Lepak, Wang, & Takeuchi, 2007). It is unclear if this is the result of the synergy through HPWS (Chadwick, 2010). Some of the items failed to yield loadings greater than 0.5 threshold; therefore, EFA led to item reduction. Six items (1, 2, 12, 15, 16, and 22) were deleted according to the results of the EFA. The items measuring selective staffing and items that emphasized "objectivity" failed to exceed the 0.5 threshold. 16 items were kept for further analyses. Cronbach's Alpha score after item purification was 0.973 indicating that the scale was reliable.

In order to measure proactive personality, Proactive Personality Scale (PPS) by Bateman and Crant (1993) was used. Eight items were selected for measurement. The items were rated on a 5-point scale ranging from 1 (definitely disagree) to 5 (definitely agree). Item loadings were above 0.5 and no item was deleted. Cronbach's Alpha implied a high reliability with a score of 0.98.

Self-leadership construct was operationalized by using the Abbreviated Self-Leadership Questionnaire (ASLQ) developed by Houghton, Dawley and DiLiello (2012). The scale consists of 9 items. The answers were rated on a 5-point Likert scale ranging from 1 (definitely disagree) to 5 (definitely agree).

The items were expected to load under three factors: namely, behavior-focused strategies, natural reward strategies and constructive thought pattern strategies; but the results revealed a 1-factor structure again. Nel and Zyl (2015) showed that the unidimensional model of the ASLQ revealed a better fitting model rather than the three-dimensional model. Regarding the psychometric properties of the questionnaire, it was concluded that it was better to conceptualize ASLQ as a single factor and self-leadership as a unidimensional construct when measured by using ASLQ (Nel & Zyl, 2015). Therefore, within the framework of this research, self-leadership was accepted as a unidimensional construct. Also, two items from the dimension constructive thought patterns – item 3 and 5 – were omitted from the analysis due to low loadings. Cronbach's Alpha score was calculated as 0.973 after item purification.

Self-efficacy perceptions of the participants were assessed by using the Generalized Self-Efficacy Scale developed by Schwarzer and Jerusalem (1995). This scale included 10 items. Items were rated on a 5-point scale ranging from 1 (definitely disagree) to 5 (definitely agree) and 3 items (1, 7, and 8) were deleted after factor analysis due to low loadings. EFA resulted in 1-factor solution as expected with a high reliability score of 0.970.

To operationalize one of the dependent variables, work engagement, Utrecht Work Engagement Scale (UWES) by Schaufeli and Bakker (2003) was used. The scale consisted of 17 items aimed to measure three dimensions: vigor, dedication and absorption. The rating scale ranged from 1 (never) to 5 (always) questioning how frequently the participant exerted the given behaviors. All item loadings were above the threshold 0.5 and therefore no items were excluded. EFA resulted in 1-factor solution contrary to expectations. Schaufeli and Bakker (2003), in their original work, state that UWES can be considered as both a one-dimensional or three-dimensional construct. Cronbach's Alpha score of the scale is found to be 0.973 and this is also considered as an indicator of the unidimensional structure. It is also mentioned that when one is interested in the construct as a whole, then it is more appropriate to accept it as a one-dimensional model (Schaufeli & Bakker, 2003).

Lastly, organizational citizenship behavior ratings are obtained from supervisors. OCBI and OCBO scales developed by Williams and Anderson (1991) were used to operationalize organizational citizenship behaviors. Both scales consist of 7 items and are rated on a 5-point scale ranging from 1 (definitely disagree) to 5 (definitely agree). There were 3 reverse items in OCBO which were, "Takes undeserved work breaks", "A great deal of his/her time is spent on personal phone/email/other communications" and "Complains about insignificant things at work". Therefore, at first, these items were recoded. OCBI and OCBO are considered as two dimensions of OCB and, therefore, the items were expected to load under 2 factors. But the first EFA revealed a 1-factor structure. Due to the fact that these dimensions are used to measure a common construct, this loading is considered as an acceptable outcome. The scales were combined and treated as one construct, namely "General Organizational Citizenship Behavior". Cronbach's Alpha coefficient yielded a score of 0.970 indicating a high level of internal reliability.

The variables and corresponding reliability statistics are summarized on the next page in Table 3.

Table 3: Measures and Reliability Statistics of the Variables in Study 1

Variable	Source	Number of Items (Original)	Number of Items (Purified)	Reliability
Transformational Leadership	Bass and Avolio (1995)	20 items	20 items	α=0.98
HPWS	Sun, Aryee, and Law (2007)	22 items	16 items	α=0.97

Variable	Source	Number of Items (Original)	Number of Items (Purified)	Reliability
Proactive Personality	Bateman and Crant (1993)	8 items	8 items	α=0.98
Self-leadership	Houghton, Dawley, and DiLiello (2012)	9 items	7 items	α=0.97
Self-efficacy	Schwarzer & Jerusalem (1995)	10 items	7 items	α=0.97
Work Engagement	Schaufeli and Bakker (2003)	17 items	17 items	α=0.97
OCB	Williams and Anderson (1991)	14 items	14 items	α=0.97

During the analyses, a common pattern of high reliability statistics for all the variables was observed. Also, all the constructs revealed a 1-factor structure. In literature, when Alpha is too high, this is evaluated as high item redundancy, meaning that a number of items target the same question in different ways. It is stated that α or Cronbach's Alpha is not only dependent on the correlations between items but also on the number of the items and adding items to the scale increases the reliability score of the scale considerably (Streiner, Norman, & Cairney, 2015). Cortina (1993) states that if the number of items in a scale is greater than 14, then this scale guarantees to reach at least 0.70 reliability level. Also, Alpha is expected to increase as the correlation between the dimensions increases. Regarding that most of the variables have many items and load under 1 factor due to high correlations among dimensions, high reliability statistics can be considered as acceptable. It suggests a unity in how the items were understood by the participants. Also, within the whole research no negatively worded item was used because of the structure of the Turkish language. Previous research suggests that inclusion of negatively worded (not reverse) items may lead to measurement errors in Turkish context (Turgut & Erden, 2013). In this respect, each scale may have been perceived as a whole without any wording related interruption.

As stated before, OCB has been perceived as a single construct and the items of OCBI and OCBO have loaded under 1 factor. Therefore, onwards, the items will be treated as a whole and OCB will not be separated. The hypotheses of the study are accordingly revised and given on the next page in Table 4.

Table 4: Revised List of Hypotheses

No.	Hypothesis
H1:	There will be a positive relationship between transformational leadership and self-leadership. As transformational leadership characteristics of supervisors increase, their employees will tend to exhibit higher levels of self-leadership skills.
H2:	There will be a positive relationship between high-performance work systems and self-leadership. As employees perceive high-performance work systems to be carried out more, they will tend to exhibit higher levels of self-leadership skills.
H3:	There will be a positive relationship between proactive personality and self-leadership. The more proactive a person is, the higher levels of self-leadership skills he/she is expected to exhibit.
H4:	There will be a positive relationship between self-leadership and work engagement. As employees exhibit more self-leadership skills, they are expected to be more engaged in work.
H5:	There will be a positive relationship between self-leadership and OCB. As employees exhibit more self-leadership skills, their organizational citizenship behaviors are expected to increase.
H6:	There will be a positive relationship between self-leadership and self-efficacy. People who exhibit higher levels of self-leadership skills, are likely to have higher levels of self-efficacy.
H7:	Self-efficacy will mediate the relationship between self-leadership and work engagement.
H8:	Self-efficacy will mediate the relationship between self-leadership and OCB.

3.3.4 Reliability and validity of the models

In this section, the reliability and validity checks for the models are given. The models include multi-item constructs; therefore, by conducting a confirmatory factor analysis (CFA), the construct validity of the models should be evaluated. In this respect, confirmatory factor analysis is conducted using Analysis of Moment Structures (AMOS) 20. The visual diagram of the measurement model is given on the next page as Figure 4.

Figure 4: Visual depiction of the measurement model

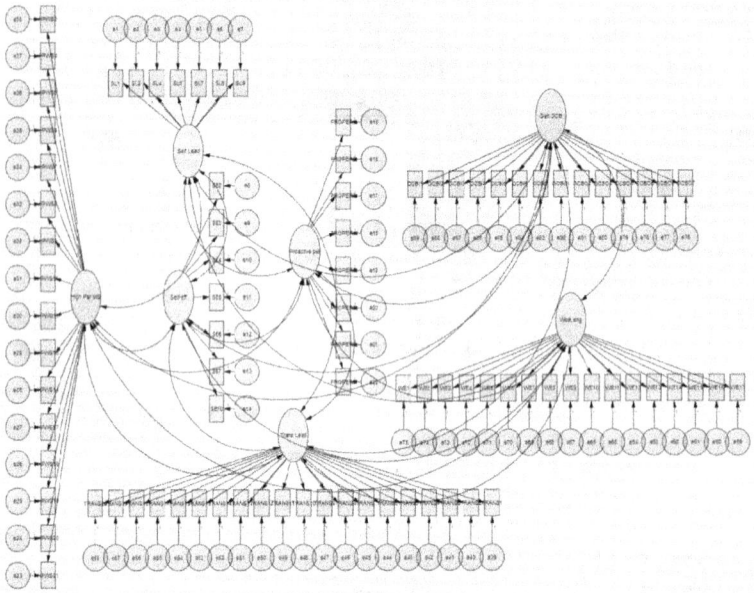

Construct validity refers to "the degree to which a construct assesses the construct it is purported to assess" (Peter, 1981, p. 134). It includes the measurement of reliability, convergent validity, discriminant validity and nomological validity. Reliability is assessed through Cronbach Alphas and composite reliability. In the previous sections, Cronbach Alphas were calculated and they all yielded acceptable results implying that the scales were internally consistent. The second indicator, composite reliability, is also used to measure the scales' internal consistency and will be calculated in this section by using the results yielded by CFA.

Reliability is a necessary but not a sufficient condition for validity; high reliability does not guarantee high validity (Raykov & Marcoulides, 2011). Therefore, the other indicators, convergent validity, discriminant validity and nomological validity should also be investigated. Convergent validity refers to the extent to which the items measuring the same construct are correlated with each other whereas discriminant validity refers to the differentiating power. Constructs measuring different phenomena should be able to distinguish between these in order to guarantee discriminant validity. Nomological validity is used to show whether anticipated relationships between constructs can be explained by theory.

Convergent validity is assessed through factor loadings, average variance extracted (AVE) and composite reliability. All factor loadings of the constructs within the model are above the statistical threshold 0.5 (Hair, Black, Babin, & Anderson, 2010). Therefore no items are eliminated. Composite reliability is calculated by dividing the squared sum of factor loadings to the squared sum of loadings plus sum of error variance terms. It indicates whether the items are able to assess the corresponding construct and the lower threshold is 0.70 (Kim et al., 2006). As seen from Table 5, all composite reliability statistics are greater than 0.70.

Table 5: Composite Reliability Values

Construct	Composite Reliability
Self-leadership	0.96
Self-efficacy	0.95
HPWS	0.95
Proactive Personality	0.95
Transformational Leadership	0.97
Work Engagement	0.97
OCB	0.96

AVE is the sum of squared standardized loadings divided by the number of items and the cut-off value is 0.5 (Hair et al., 2010). As seen from Table 6, all AVE values are greater than 0.5 indicating convergent validity.

Table 6: Squared Correlation Coefficients and AVEs

AVE	SL	SE	HPWS	PP	TL	WE	OCB
Self-leadership	0.84						
Self-efficacy	0.82	0.83					
HPWS	0.68	0.65	0.69				
Proactive Personality	0.79	0.81	0.62	0.84			
Transformational Leadership	0.69	0.64	0.68	0.56	0.72		
Work Engagement	0.68	0.67	0.64	0.67	0.56	0.68	
OCB	0.67	0.67	0.67	0.62	0.65	0.65	0.69

In order to assess discriminant validity, variance extracted estimates should be greater than the squared correlation estimates; it means AVE for each construct should be greater than its shared variance with other constructs (Fornell & Larcker, 1981). In Table 6, the diagonal values represent the AVEs and the other values are the squared correlation estimates between the other constructs. All the AVEs are greater than the squared correlations indicating that discriminant validity is also achieved.

As mentioned before, nomological validity assesses whether the anticipated relationships are compatible with theory. Therefore, high correlations are expected among the theoretically related constructs. As seen from Table 7, self-leadership is highly correlated with its anticipated determinants and outcomes, and, these relationships are probable with regard to previous literature. In this respect, nomological validity is also achieved.

Table 7: Correlation Coefficients Matrix

Correlations	SL	SE	HPWS	PP	TL	WE	OCB
Self-leadership	1						
Self-efficacy	0.88	1					
HPWS	0.81	0.78	1				
Proactive Personality	0.87	0.87	0.77	1			
Transformational Leadership	0.81	0.78	0.81	0.74	1		
Work Engagement	0.85	0.79	0.78	0.80	0.74	1	
OCB	0.79	0.80	0.79	0.77	0.78	0.79	1

All correlations are significant at 0.01 level (2-tailed).

CFA is also conducted to assess the "goodness of fit" of the measurement model. There are some basic indices that test the fit of the model and the respective threshold values. The relative chi-square index which is chi-square divided by degrees of freedom is demonstrated as CMIN/df in AMOS. The threshold value for that index is considered as 2; values less than 2 are accepted as signs of good fit (Ullman, 2001). In our model it is found to be 1.692 indicating that the model is acceptable. Comparative fit index (CFI) which is used to identify the discrepancy between the measurement model and the null model is acceptable when the values approach 1. In our model the value is 0.913 and that indicates a good fit. Tucker Lewis Index (TLI) is another index for assessing model fit and values greater than 0.90 are usually considered acceptable. The root mean square error of approximation (RMSEA) and root means square residual (RMR) are other indicators of fit. These are respectively 0.052 and 0.045 for our hypothesized model. These values are below the cut-off value and, therefore, are also regarded as acceptable (Hu & Bentler, 1999). The fit indices can be found in Table 8 alongside the threshold values.

Table 8: Fit Indices of the Measurement Model

Index	Value	Threshold Value
CMIN/df	1.692	<2
CFI	0.913	>0.90
TLI	0.910	>0.90
RMSEA	0.052	<0.06
RMR	0.045	<0.08

3.4 Data analyses and hypotheses testing

In this part, the data analyses for Study 1 are conducted. First, the descriptive statistics regarding the constructs are given. Then, the hypotheses are tested using IBM Statistical Package for Social Sciences (IBM SPSS) 22. Multiple regression and hierarchical regression analyses are conducted in order to test the relevant hypotheses.

Table 9 summarizes the descriptive statistics regarding the constructs. It is seen that the means of each construct are above 3.00; proactive personality and organizational citizenship being the highest with a mean of 3.81 whereas work engagement is the lowest with a mean of 3.62.

Table 9: Descriptive Statistics – Study 1

	Minimum	Maximum	Mean	Standard Deviation
Transformational Leadership	1.20	5.00	3.77	.95
HPWS	1.23	5.00	3.74	.95
Proactive Personality	1.00	5.00	3.81	1.20
Self-leadership	1.00	5.00	3.76	1.16
Self-efficacy	1.00	5.00	3.80	1.16
Work engagement	1.24	5.00	3.62	.86
OCB	1.42	5.00	3.81	.90

3.4.1 Study 1 – Model testing (1)

In this first model, we hypothesize that transformational leadership, high-performance work systems and proactive personality positively influence self-leadership (H1, H1 and H3 respectively) as indicated in Figure 5. In order to test these hypotheses, least-squares multiple regression analysis is conducted.

Figure 5: Model 1

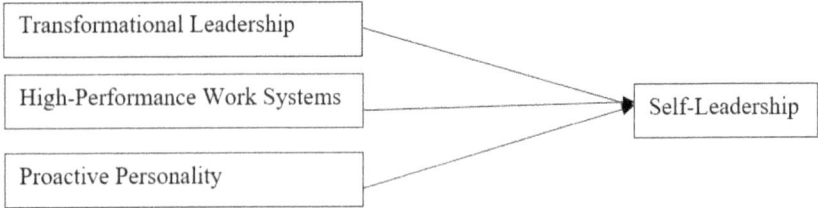

As independent variables, transformational leadership, high-performance work systems and proactive personality, as dependent variable self-leadership and as control variables age, gender, education level and industry are included in the model.

The regression analyses were conducted in two steps: first, the control variables were entered and then, the independent variables were added in order to see the change in R square. The results of the regression analyses can be found in Table 10 and Table 11.

Table 10: Results of the Least-squares Multiple Regression Analysis for Self-leadership – Model 1

Model Summary					
Model	R	R Square	Adjusted R Square	Std. Error of the Estimate	Durbin-Watson
1	.23[a]	.05	.04	1.14	
2	.91[b]	.84	.84	.46	1.80

a. Predictors: (Constant), Education, Gender, Age, Industry
b. Predictors: (Constant), Education, Gender, Age, Industry, HPWS, Proactive Personality, Transformational Leadership

Table 11: Regression Coefficients for Self-leadership – Model 1

Coefficients[a]							
Model	Unstandardized Coefficients		Standardized Coefficients	t	Sig.	Collinearity Statistics	
	B	Std. Error	Beta			Tolerance	VIF
1 (Constant)	4.84	.46		10.49	.00		
Industry	.09	.10	.06	.98	.32	.88	1.12
Age	-.26	.09	-.17	-2.72	.00	.90	1.10
Gender	-.06	.14	-.02	-.41	.68	.98	1.01
Education	-.39	.12	-.21	-3.26	.00	.88	1.12
2 (Constant)	-.16	.24		-.68	.49		
Industry	.09	.04	.05	2.20	.02	.87	1.14
Age	-.03	.04	-.02	-.78	.43	.87	1.14
Gender	-.01	.06	-.00	-.28	.77	.95	1.04
Education	-.13	.05	-.07	-2.62	.00	.85	1.17
ProactivePers	.47	.04	.49	11.83	.00	.36	2.74
HPWS	.35	.06	.29	5.70	.00	.24	4.15
Transform Lead	.24	.06	.19	3.99	.00	.26	3.84

a. Dependent Variable: Self-leadership

The results show that the second model is able to explain 84% of the variance in self-leadership (R^2=0.84; F=194.008; p=0.000). When proactive personality, HPWS and transformational leadership are added to the base model, R square has increased from 0.05 to 0.84. High-performance work systems (B=0.29, p<.05), transformational leadership (B=0.19, p<.05) and proactive personality (B=0.49, p<.05) are found to contribute to self-leadership significantly, providing support for H1, H2 and H3 respectively. Besides that, industry (B=0.05, p<.05) and education level (B=-0.07, p<.05) are found to have an effect over self-leadership. Different industries are found to affect self-leadership differently and there is a negative relationship between educational level and self-leadership. As educational level increases, self-leadership is found to decrease.

3.4.2 Study 1 – Model testing (2)

In the second model, it is hypothesized that self-leadership will contribute to work engagement and organizational citizenship behavior through increasing self-efficacy. Figure 6 depicts these anticipated relationships. It is asserted that self-leadership will have a positive effect on work engagement (H4), on organizational citizenship behavior (H5), and on self-efficacy (H6). The mediation hypotheses suggest that self-efficacy will mediate the relationship between self-leadership and work engagement (H7); and between self-leadership and organizational citizenship behavior (H8). In order to test these hypotheses, Baron and Kenny's (1986) three step regression analyses are conducted.

Figure 6: Model 2

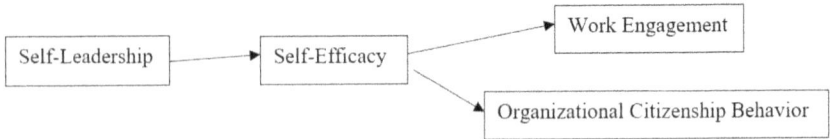

Three consecutive regression analyses are performed for each dependent variable. Table 12 shows the results of the analyses performed for work engagement.

Table 12: Regression Analyses for Work Engagement

Model	R^2	R^2_{adj}	Sig.	F		B	Sig.
1	0.64	0.64	0.00	464.607			
					Self-leadership	0.80	0.00
Dependent Variable: Work Engagement Independent Variable: Self-leadership							
2	0.85	0.85	0.00	701.696			
					Self-leadership	0.92	0.00
Dependent Variable: Self-efficacy Independent Variable: Self-leadership							
3	0.73	0.73	0.00	350.892			
Dependent Variable: Work Engagement Independent Variable: Self-leadership, Self-efficacy							
					Self-leadership	0.07	0.38
					Self-efficacy	0.78	0.00

In Baron and Kenny's (1986) procedure, there should be a significant relationship between the independent and dependent; between the independent and mediator; and the effect of the independent variable should no longer be significant when entered into the regression together with the mediator in order to speak of full mediation. Therefore, in the first model, self-leadership is regressed on work engagement. H4 hypothesized that there will be a positive relationship between self-leadership and work engagement. As employees exhibit more self-leadership skills, they are expected to be more engaged in work. As expected, the results show that self-leadership positively contributes to work engagement (B=0.80, p<.05) providing support for H4. In the second model, the effect of self-leadership on self-efficacy is investigated. It is seen that self-leadership has a positive effect on self-efficacy (B=0.92, p<.05), providing support for H6 which hypothesized a positive relationship between self-leadership and self-efficacy. People who exhibit higher levels of self-leadership skills are likely to have higher levels of self-efficacy. In the last step, self-leadership and self-efficacy, both, are entered into the model as independent variables in order to test H7 which hypothesized that self-efficacy will mediate the relationship between self-leadership and work engagement. The coefficient of self-leadership is no longer significant (B=0.07, p=0.38) whereas self-efficacy has a significant effect on work engagement (B=0.78, p<.05). This provides support for H7 indicating that self-efficacy fully mediates the relationship between self-leadership and work engagement.

After that, the same procedure is followed for organizational citizenship behavior. The results of the regression analyses are presented in Table 13.

Table 13: Regression Analyses for OCB

Model	R^2	R^2_{adj}	Sig.	F		B	Sig.
1	0.63	0.63	0.00	448.870			
					Self-leadership	0.79	0.00
Dependent Variable: OCB Independent Variable: Self-leadership							
2	0.85	0.85	0.00	546.861			
					Self-leadership	0.92	0.00
Dependent Variable: Self-efficacy Independent Variable: Self-leadership							
3	0.68	0.68	0.00	282.791			
Dependent Variable: OCB Independent Variable: Self-leadership, Self-efficacy							
					Self-leadership	0.23	0.01
					Self-efficacy	0.60	0.00

At first, self-leadership is regressed on OCB in order to test H5 which suggested that there will be a positive relationship between self-leadership and OCB. As employees exhibit more self-leadership skills, their organizational citizenship behaviors are expected to increase. The results show that self-leadership positively contributes to OCB (B=0.79, p<.05) providing support for H5. In the second model, the effect of self-leadership on self-efficacy is again observed (B=0.92, p<.05). Lastly, self-leadership and self-efficacy are regressed on OCB to test H8 which hypothesized that self-efficacy will mediate the relationship between self-leadership and OCB. Although the Beta coefficient of self-leadership has dropped from 0.92 to 0.23, the coefficient is still significant (p<.05). Therefore, it is not possible to state that there is a full mediation. We see that the significance level (p value) has also decreased from 0.00 to 0.01. Therefore, it can be concluded that self-efficacy partially mediates the relationship between self-leadership and OCB, and therefore, H8 is partially supported. The results of the hypotheses tests are indicated on the next page in Table 14.

Table 14: Result of Hypotheses Testing

No.	Hypothesis	Result
H1:	There will be a positive relationship between transformational leadership and self-leadership. As transformational leadership characteristics of supervisors increase, their employees will tend to exhibit higher levels of self-leadership skills.	Supported
H2:	There will be a positive relationship between high-performance work systems and self-leadership. As employees perceive high-performance work systems to be carried out more, they will tend to exhibit higher levels of self-leadership skills.	Supported
H3:	There will be a positive relationship between proactive personality and self-leadership. The more proactive a person is, the higher levels of self-leadership skills he/she is expected to exhibit.	Supported
H4:	There will be a positive relationship between self-leadership and work engagement. As employees exhibit more self-leadership skills, they are expected to be more engaged in work.	Supported
H5:	There will be a positive relationship between self-leadership and OCB. As employees exhibit more self-leadership skills, their organizational citizenship behaviors are expected to increase.	Supported
H6:	There will be a positive relationship between self-leadership and self-efficacy. People who exhibit higher levels of self-leadership skills, are likely to have higher levels of self-efficacy.	Supported
H7:	Self-efficacy will mediate the relationship between self-leadership and work engagement.	Supported
H8:	Self-efficacy will mediate the relationship between self-leadership and OCB.	Partially Supported

3.4.3 Analyses regarding demographics

In this part, the effect of some demographic variables on self-leadership will be examined. Independent groups t test and analysis of variance (ANOVA) are used to investigate differences.

First, gender is taken into account. Independent samples t test is used to see whether self-leadership shows a significant difference according to gender. The results of the t test are given in Table 15.

Table 15: T test for Gender

	Levene's Test for Equality of Variances	
Self-leadership	**F**	**Sig.**
Equal variances assumed	.17	.67
Equal variances not assumed		

The results show that there is no significant difference between males and females in terms of their self-leadership levels (p>.05). Mean self-leadership for males is calculated as 3.75 whereas the mean for females is found to be 3.82.

In order to see whether self-leadership changes according to age, tenure in work life and tenure in current organization, correlation analyses are applied. The results can be seen in Table 16.

Table 16: Correlation Analyses for Age and Tenure

Correlations		Self Leadership	Age	Tenure in Company	Tenure in Work Life
Self Leadership	Pearson Correlation	1			
	Sig. (2-tailed)				
	N	258			
Age	Pearson Correlation	-.13*	1		
	Sig. (2-tailed)	.03			
	N	258	258		
Tenure in Company	Pearson Correlation	-.12*	.68**	1	
	Sig. (2-tailed)	.04	.00		
	N	258	258	258	

Correlations				
	Self Leadership	Age	Tenure in Company	Tenure in Work Life
Tenure in Work Life — Pearson Correlation	-.05	.87**	.67**	1
Sig. (2-tailed)	.35	.00	.00	
N	258	258	258	258

*. Correlation is significant at the 0.05 level (2-tailed).
**. Correlation is significant at the 0.01 level (2-tailed).

According to the table, there are some significant but weak correlations among variables. Age has a negative correlation with self-leadership, indicating that as age increases, self-leadership tends to decrease. Tenure in work life has no significant correlation with self-leadership whereas tenure in company has a negative correlation. As the tenure in a company increases, self-leadership tends to decrease.

For education level, the participants are grouped under 3 categories. In the original survey form, there were 4 groups including graduate level. Since there are only 2 people in this category, it is combined with Bachelor level and the analyses are conducted accordingly. ANOVA is performed in order to see if variances are equal. As we see from the table the null hypothesis that variances are equal is rejected; there is a significant difference among groups. Therefore, as post-hoc analysis, Tamhane is conducted and the differences are examined. Table 17 and Table 18 show the results of the analyses. It is seen that there is a gap between self-leadership levels of the participants with higher educational levels – group 3 and high school graduates – group 2 (see Table 17 and Table 18).

Table 17: ANOVA Results for Education Level

ANOVA					
Self-leadership					
	Sum of Squares	Df	Mean Square	F	Sig.
Between Groups	17.776	2	8.88	6.792	.00
Within Groups	333.691	255	1.30		
Total	351.466	257			

Table 18: Self-leadership Means According to Education Level

	N	Mean	Std. Deviation	Std. Error
Secondary School	42	3.89	1.15	.18
High School	160	3.92	1.04	.08
University and Higher	56	3.28	1.40	.19
Total	258	3.78	1.17	.07

Lastly, the demographic variable of interest is the industry. Industry is categorized under 4 groups: food and beverage, retail, customer services and financial services. There are only 10 participants working in financial services sector: therefore, as the sample size is smaller than 30, Kruskal-Wallis test is used.

The results show that there is a significant difference among industries in terms of self-leadership of employees. Table 19 depicts the mean self-leadership levels across industries. It is seen that financial services industry has the greatest mean among all the industries whereas customer services sector has the lowest.

Table 19: Self- leadership Means Across Industries

	N	Mean	Std. Deviation	Std. Error
Food and Beverage	49	3.72	1.22	.17
Retail	138	3.90	1.03	.09
Customer Services	61	3.38	1.38	.17
Financial Services	10	4.70	.14	.04
Total	258	3.78	1.17	.07

Chapter 4 Study 2 – Qualitative exploration of determinants and outcomes of self-leadership

Abstract: Self-leadership has gained attention from scholars and practitioners in that it has paved the way for substituting the leader. Although all leadership theories have added a deeper understanding to the leadership literature, most of them have failed to grasp the importance of followers. Self-leadership, in this respect, has turned the eyes from the leader to the other side and has drawn attention to the unutilized potential of the followers.

It has been shown that self-leadership has a positive effect on job outcomes such as job satisfaction, commitment, trust and performance (Neck & Houghton, 2006; Neck & Manz, 1996). Despite its importance, self-leadership research has generally gathered around dispositional factors that precede self-leadership and especially around the correlation between Big Five Personality Traits and self-leadership (e.g., Houghton et al., 2004; Williams, 1997). Literature on the contextual determinants has been limited to training and reward systems (Stewart et al., 2011). In this respect, the understanding of the situational factors that can contribute to the development of self-leadership skills required being deepened.

Study 1 has shown us that contextual factors such as high-performance work systems and transformational leadership have a significant contribution to self-leadership and are able to explain an important part of the variance in self-leadership. This has provided evidence for the effect of contextual factors on self-leadership. In this respect, targeting that, Study 2 aims to find out other possible contextual determinants and outcomes of self-leadership. In Study 2, this is taken further to question if any other contextual factors can influence the use of self-leadership skills positively or negatively. In Study 1, it has also been shown that self-leadership has a positive effect on employee outcomes – organizational citizenship behavior and work engagement. In Study 2, it is also aimed to find out other possible outcomes of self-leadership. In this respect, in-depth interviews are conducted. Two major research questions were addressed:

– What other contextual factors can contribute to/hinder self-leadership skills?
– What other employee outcomes are affected from self-leadership?

In this chapter, first, the methodology of Study 2 will be indicated, Sample quotations will also be given and results will be presented. The findings will be discussed further in Section 5.1 in correspondence with the results of Study 1.

4.1 Research design and methodology

In this section, the data collection process and methodology of Study 2 will be discussed and sample characteristics will be explained.

4.1.1 Sampling and data collection

Study 2 consists of 13 semi-structured interviews conducted with 6 men and 7 women. The interviews lasted 5 to 15 minutes and were tape-recorded. The answers were transcribed verbatim. The questions were asked to find out which factors could contribute to/hinder self-leadership and what possible outcomes self-leadership could lead to. After decoding, the interviews were content analyzed.

The interview form consists of two parts. At the first part, questions regarding the factors that facilitate/hinder self-leadership are investigated with 6 questions. The first questions address the actual conditions that affect self-leadership whereas the others address the hypothetical circumstances that are expected to affect the phenomenon. The second part includes demographic questions.

4.1.2 Sample characteristics

The sample consists of 6 men and 7 women. The ages of the participants vary between 24 and 38. Most of the interviewees have experience in work life less than 5 years (46%). The tenure in current organization is also less than 5 years for 92% of the participants. They work in different sectors including chemical, education, energy, finance etc. The demographics are indicated in Table 20.

Table 20: Sample Demographics of Study 2

Characteristic	Category	Frequency	Percent
Gender	Men	6	46%
	Women	7	54%
Age	20–25	3	23%
	26–30	3	23%
	30–35	6	46%
	36–40	1	8%
Tenure in Work Life	Up to 5 years	6	46%
	6–10 years	5	38%
	11–15 years	2	16%
Tenure in Current Organization	Up to 5 years	12	92%
	6–10 years	1	8%
Education Level	University	5	38%
	Masters	8	62%

Characteristic	Category	Frequency	Percent
Sector	Chemical	2	16%
	Education	1	8%
	Energy	3	23%
	Finance	1	8%
	Food and Beverage	1	8%
	Insurance	2	16%
	Transportation	1	8%
	Advertising	1	8%
	Furniture	1	8%

4.2 Results of study 2

The interviews were conducted to see whether the findings complement the results of Study 1 and to gain a deeper understanding of other possible antecedents and consequences of self-leadership. In this respect, 6 questions were asked (except demographics). The first question examined the level of self-leadership that the individuals used in their current jobs. It was asked in order to enable the participants to think about their own behaviors and cognitions and to see whether a variance is valid in terms of self-leadership levels of participants. The second question addressed the factors that contributed to the use of self-leadership skills whereas the third one addressed the factors that hindered self-leadership. Parallel to that, the fourth and fifth questions respectively targeted other possible facilitators and possible blockers of self-leadership that the individual could add. The last question was asked to see the outcomes of self-leadership.

First of all, the factors/practices that contribute to self-leadership were questioned. The interviewees stated different opinions. Autonomy/initiative, recognition, feeling trusted, customer satisfaction, recognition, incentive reward, results-oriented appraisal, internal mobility and competition were expressed to facilitate self-leadership.

The results indicate that 7 of the 13 (54%) interviewees mentioned mostly autonomy/taking initiative or responsibility as an antecedent of self-leadership. Sample quotations are given below:

> Interviewee 8: "As a team, we decide how we do our jobs and who does what. That's very important for me. Also, the company sends us to different plants all over the world and we follow the work there. It gives us the opportunity to track and control the processes on our own".

Interviewee 13: "Another factor is being free. Being able to plan my work myself, and being able to determine my priorities".

Interviewee 10: "Sometimes I do extra discounts or I exert more effort to sell. This initiative is given to me".

Interviewee 7: "Besides that, when a task is given to me, I don't like being interfered. If the task is mine, then I should also be given the freedom to determine how it's conducted".

Interviewee 6: "With regard to my job description, I am the only one responsible for my region. This helps me to improve my self-leadership".

Interviewee 4: "If I am the only one responsible for the task, I set goals for myself to accomplish it quickly".

Interviewee 9: "Another factor is working individually. When I work alone and not depend on others, I think I plan my tasks better. Otherwise everyone can interfere in everything".

Some interviewees mentioned that the tasks they perform should be observable and appreciated by their colleagues and/or supervisors. This is regarded as "recognition" and the sample quotations are indicated below. Two of the 13 (15%) participants implied that recognition contributed to the development of self-leadership skills.

Interviewee 4: "The most motivating factor among all is to be known as a hardworking person. What I do should be observable by my colleagues and supervisors".

Interviewee 7: "That the work I do is seen and appreciated by my supervisor is very important for me to motivate myself".

Two (15%) of the interviewees mentioned that feeling trusted by their supervisors was the major driver for them in exerting self-leadership skills.

Interviewee 8: "The company trusts us. I guess, these are the most nourishing factors".

Interviewee 10: "First of all comes trust. The manager leaves the store to me and I am so afraid that I will disappoint him. I don't want to let him down".

Customer satisfaction is suggested as another factor that has a positive effect over self-leadership. Two of the interviewees (15%) asserted that customer feedback was important.

Interviewee 7: "Another factor is customer satisfaction. Customer satisfaction forms a performance criterion for me".

Interviewee 10: "Also you can understand what the customers think. When you do not care for their concerns and they are disappointed, you can sense it. It is an immediate reflection. Therefore, I try to concentrate on the work better".

In line with HPWS dimension-incentive rewards, monetary gains are mentioned as another factor that can lead the employees to lead themselves. Three of the interviewees (23%) mentioned rewards as a facilitator for self-leadership.

Interviewee 7: "Monetary reward is also important for me to aim for better".

Interviewee 3: "Also, my self-leadership is increased through the use of rewards/bonuses within the framework of company policy".

Interviewee 13: "What motivates me is money. I take into account what I get. I try to get rewards and money".

Observable and measurable performance appraisal and feedback are mentioned by 2 of the interviewees (15%) to be another important factor in facilitating self-leadership. The answers correspond with the "results-oriented appraisal" dimension of HPWS.

Interviewee 3: "It is helpful that the tasks are measurable and reported because it enables to see the quality and the positive and negative sides of the job clearly".

Interviewee 4: "In our company there are performance interviews and rating systems. Every year our manager gives us feedback on the previous year regarding our progress. You can get higher ratings when you improve your work according to these feedbacks".

In line with HPWS dimension – "internal mobility" – an interviewee (8%) expressed promotion opportunities to be a facilitator.

Interviewee 11: "I think that the firm is convenient for promotion. Because, there is only one manager and the rest is generally people with junior positions; at least in my department, I directly report to the highest level. Therefore I see my future bright".

The last factor expressed during the interviews was competition. Two of the interviewees (15%) told that competition enhanced their use of self-leadership skills.

Interviewee 9: "The first thing I can say is competition. As the competition increases, I do anything to get my performance to a higher level. In the end everyone's aim is to be promoted. Therefore you have to make yourself realized".

Interviewee 12: "This sector is a harsh one. You have to be very creative to survive. Therefore, I can say that the competition keeps me alive. It helps me to aim for better. I have to be at least one step ahead of my rivals".

After that, the factors/practices that hindered the use of self-leadership skills were investigated. The answers yielded a set of variables, some of which overlap with the answers in the previous question. The interviewees mentioned that lack of recognition, competition, autonomy, being trusted and training opportunities affected their self-leadership negatively. An ineffective manager was also identified as a negative influence. Besides that, unclear job descriptions and negative perceptions of distributive justice were also seen to have a negative effect on the exertion of self-leadership.

Negative perceptions of distributive justice take the lead with a 23%. Three of the 13 interviewees mentioned this as a factor that blunted their self-leadership skills.

Interviewee 8: "I would be better to say so: When someone who is less experienced than me earns the same amount as me, I start to question. Then I cannot see any reason to perform better".

Interviewee 7: "It is the same for things like bonus and wage. When I see that people exert less effort than me but are rewarded more, then it feels meaningless to increase my performance".

Interviewee 2: "I don't think that I get what I deserve".

Lack of autonomy was also mentioned by 2 of the interviewees (15%) to have a negative effect.

Interviewee 7: "As I've mentioned before, being interfered and being not appreciated decreases my motivation".

Interviewee 11: "When I try to take initiative, I am confronted with negative reactions. At those times, I am told that I should not decide and act by myself".

Lack of trust was another factor that was mentioned during the interviews by an interviewee (8%).

Interviewee 7: "Especially I expect that my supervisors trust me when I do a job. When this trust environment is not provided, I lose my enthusiasm and see no reason to do better".

Lack of training and development opportunities were also mentioned by one participant (8%) to affect self-leadership corresponding to the HPWS dimension of "extensive training".

Interviewee 2: "Employee satisfaction is not important in my company. There are no personal development programs and we cannot use our potential".

An ineffective managerial style was also stated to hinder self-leadership skills. The interviewees used adjectives such as "strict" or "bad" to define their managers. What is meant by "strict/bad" is further questioned. Three of the 13 participants (23%) agreed that an ineffective manager affected their self-leadership negatively.

Interviewee 1: "A bad management style, first of all. What I mean is that managers should treat their employees fairly and should be able to lead them. But, here, my manager behaves in a way that decreases my motivation, sometimes it can even be named as mobbing. Managers should be one step ahead of their employees".

Interviewee 13: "That the manager does not know what I do and tries to supervise me and determine my priorities affect all of my outcomes, in a negative way. Good managers try to supply you with the required resources, to remove the hurdles in your way, to create the connections you need, or try to advertise your project if successfully completed, they "sell" your project and protect you".

Interviewee 3: "Working with unsuccessful managers hinders my skills. In my opinion, a manager who cannot communicate effectively, who does not follow up the work given to employees and who has a big ego that prevents him from admitting his faults is a bad manager".

With regard to recognition, a participant (8%) expressed the following ideas.

Interviewee 9: "It's not clear who does what. What I mean is that, when you do something with others, there is always someone who does nothing but eats the pie. In this kind of situation my effort is not realized and appreciated. And that affects me negatively".

An interviewee (8%) mentioned unclear job descriptions to have a negative effect over self-leadership skills.

Interviewee 12: "That the work I do is very irrelevant to what I should do and that my job description is unclear".

The last factor that was mentioned by one participant (8%) was lack of competition.

Interviewee 10: "It would be better if there was competition. Lack of competition hinders my skills. I am the best within the store and even the region. I see from the sales numbers in fairs".

After these questions, the hypothetical part took start. The interviewees were asked to state what kind of an environment could develop or blunt their self-leadership skills. Possible facilitators that were mentioned by interviewees included organizational culture/structure, recognition, extensive training, manager capabilities, autonomy, justice, clear job descriptions and internal mobility.

Answers regarding culture/climate were indicated by 3 interviewees (23%) to be possible drivers of self-leadership. The quotations are given below:

Interviewee 2: "An environment in which I feel valuable, I feel my opinions are appreciated, my concerns are answered and I take what I deserve".

Interviewee 3: "A positive atmosphere with a high energy".

Interviewee 11: "I guess a more horizontal structure is required for the development of self-leadership because you don't need to climb to the upper levels. Communicating more easily with these levels will both enable the organization to act faster and you to do more in less time. In this respect, I think horizontal structures are required for self-leadership to develop".

In line with this, the managerial style was also mentioned by 3 interviewees (23%) as an effective factor.

Interviewee 3: "The supervisor should have the characteristics of a successful manager".

Interviewee 11: "I think, here, the experience of the managers is also crucial. With the help of this experience they can predict what their employees can or cannot do and it will be easier for them to lead".

Interviewee 7: "Fairness, a just management".

Training and development opportunities or "extensive training" were anticipated as possible facilitators by 3 of the participants (23%).

Interviewee 1: "A company that continuously improved me with training programs could be better".

Interviewee 10: "I should know the sector, the equipment, the consumer. I should not stay speechless when a question comes. Therefore it would be better if they organized training programs".

Interviewee 5: "An environment that supported individual development".

Results-oriented appraisal was expressed as an important factor by 3 interviewees (23%).

Interviewee 9: "As I mentioned, a system that shows my contribution clearly is required. Eventually what determines everything is your performance. I would not want to endeavor in vain".

Interviewee 5: "An environment that evaluated really according to performance".

Interviewee 7: "Getting my efforts' worth both financially and emotionally".

As mentioned in previous parts, autonomy was again expressed as an important contextual determinant by 3 of the interviewees (23%).

Interviewee 7: "...being provided with autonomy in terms of doing my job, these are the first things that come to my mind".

Interviewee 8: "And being given the flexibility to do my job, being authorized".

Interviewee 13: "In an environment that I have no resource scarcity and I am left free it would flourish. What I mean by resource is being able to decide based on my own plans without considering constraints such as labor, machine, equipment and without being interrupted. But when everything is limited and everything I do is questioned, my success and my motivation go down".

Mentioned as a whole, justice perceptions go in line with organizational culture and management style. In terms of justice, 4 participants (31%) gave the following hints.

Interviewee 7: "Fairness, a just management, getting my efforts' worth both financially and emotionally, being provided with autonomy in terms of doing my job, these are the first things that come to my mind".

Interviewee 12: "It would be helpful to work in equal circumstances with equal workloads".

Interviewee 11: "Also, a manager should not promote according to personal relationships. A friend of mine lived that. His manager promoted somebody else with whom his personal contact was good although my friend deserved it. These promotions should be transparent and controllable".

Interviewee 8: "A fair work environment in which I get what I deserve".

Promotion opportunities and clear career paths were mentioned to be crucial by 2 interviewees (15%). What these answers mention is in line with the internal mobility dimension of HPWS.

Interviewee 4: "A department in which I could be promoted would be very effective".

Interviewee 8: "Knowing where I will be in a couple of years is important for me".

Clear job descriptions were identified as a facilitator by one interviewee (8%).

Interviewee 12: "The most important is that my job description should be clear. That means what I do should be clear".

The answers regarding the possible blockers of self-leadership include topics as task characteristics, organizational culture, results-oriented appraisal, ineffective managerial style, justice perceptions, lack of autonomy and competition.

In terms of performance appraisal, the answers showed that the lack of an objective, standardized performance system was expected to affect the use of self-leadership strategies negatively. Two of the participants (15%) emphasized that without a results-oriented appraisal system, their tendency to exert self-leadership skills would diminish.

Interviewee 1: "An environment in which success cannot be measured. If there are no objective, measurable, visible performance standards, it would hinder my self-leadership skills".

Interviewee 7: "…inequality and unfairness in performance appraisal…"

An ineffective manager was expressed as a negative factor by 5 participants (38%).

Interviewee 8: "To me, manager should lead instead of dictating. Therefore, I think, in today's climate tough managers affect employees negatively".

Interviewee 13: "…And mostly the manager. If the manager intrudes too much, it does not matter whether he has knowledge over what I do or not, if he does micromanagement, my self-leadership skills would die down".

Interviewee 5: "A strict manager that wants to control everything".

Interviewee 7: "Injustice, a rough management style… In order for the motivation to be high, a good team and a considerate manager are required, I think".

Interviewee 4: "I would not want to work with a manager who does not give feedback and support what I do".

Lack of autonomy was expressed as a possible blocker for self-leadership by 5 participants (38%).

Interviewee 9: "Depending on others, consulting someone for every detail would affect me negatively. I should have decision making initiative in some topics".

Interviewee 11: "An environment with lots of rules and boundaries, with high hierarchy and no room for initiative would hinder self-leadership because, in this situation, no reward would be given for your efforts".

Interviewee 8: "Having someone that interfered in my job for every detail would affect me negatively".

Interviewee 13: "But when everything is limited and everything I do is questioned, my success and my motivation go down".

Interviewee 4: "Working with a manager who interrupts in everything I do would hinder my skills".

Four (31%) interviewees mentioned the effect of culture or atmosphere on their self-leadership skills. The answers run as follows.

Interviewee 1: "A company that had no room for young brains and new ideas. I mean a classical approach for management. Like the 60s. A company that is behind the times".

Interviewee 5: "An oppressive environment in which I cannot speak up would affect me negatively".

Interviewee 7: "…the work atmosphere being bad in fact".

Interviewee 2: "Feeling invaluable. An atmosphere in which everything is valued in terms of work; everything is bureaucratic, no space for new things or change. Where I feel reluctant to express my ideas".

Task characteristics were mentioned by 3 of the interviewees (23%).

Interviewee 6: "A routine job that only deals with numbers".

Interviewee 8: "The task I do is also important. For example, the more challenging the task is, the better it is, doing the same things permanently would hinder my self-leadership".

Interviewee 9: "And also I would not want to work in an environment in which standard tasks are done and there is no competition. Both the job and the colleagues should be tough so that one can develop himself".

Another possible factor that could decrease self-leadership was specified as justice perceptions by one interviewee (8%).

Interviewee 7: "Injustice ...inequality and unfairness in performance appraisal..."

The last factor mentioned was lack of competition. A participant (8%) stated that unless a competitive environment is established, self-leadership skills would diminish.

Interviewee 9: "And also I would not want to work in environment in which standard tasks are done and there is no competition. Both the job and the colleagues should be though so that one can develop himself".

Regarding the answers related to the outcomes of self-leadership, the statements pointed at increased performance, self-confidence, self-development, work engagement, and effective stress and time management.

The mostly mentioned outcome was increased performance/success or productivity with 9 interviewees mentioning it (69%).

Interviewee 1: "That brings me higher performance".

Interviewee 11: "With the experiences you get, you are able to think twice in the future. They act as a guide and enable you to take a better step. And consequently this increases my performance".

Interviewee 9: "When I do an individual task, I think its quality increases. Eventually what I aim is to produce better than others, even better than myself. Especially when I reach what I want, I ask why not better. In this regard my performance increases with these strategies".

Interviewee 4: "Being a good, successful employee and self-development".

Interviewee 3: "As it helps to develop personally and professionally, it brings along success".

Interviewee 8: "Establishing performance goals facilitates actualizing it".

Interviewee 7: "Setting goals for myself, first of all, enables me to manage myself and I can carry out my tasks orderly. And naturally, I think that I exhibit a better performance".

Interviewee 12: "I know my goals and act accordingly. I can motivate myself to perform better even if there is no extrinsic motivation sources".

Interviewee 5: "It increases my productivity".

In terms of self-development 3 interviewees (23%) made the following remarks.

Interviewee 13: "I can develop myself accordingly for my career".

Interviewee 7: "Before anything else, it helps to develop myself. Since I always try to ascend my previous standard, I can produce more effective and creative solutions".

Interviewee 3: "As it helps to develop personally and professionally, it brings along success".

Self-confidence was another concept that was expressed by 2 of the participants (15%).

Interviewee 6: "I can say that it increases my self-confidence".

Interviewee 8: "When I reach my goals, my self-confidence increases and I'm motivated to achieve more".

Some answers emphasized "enjoying the work". These were accepted as referring to work engagement. Three of the interviewees (23%) stated that they were more engaged in their work.

Interviewee 7: "When I have successful results and I am appreciated, the pleasure I get from my work automatically increases too".

Interviewee 10: "When I feel that I give the work its due, I feel better. When the consumer is satisfied, I enjoy the work I do".

Interviewee 3: "In the long term, it helps to do my job with pleasure and enthusiasm".

Finally, 2 interviewees (15%) mentioned that self-leadership enabled them to cope with stress more easily and to manage time better.

Interviewee 5: "I can handle stress better".

Interviewee 7: "I can say that it also contributes in terms of time management. Setting goals for myself, first of all, enables me to manage myself and I can carry out my tasks orderly".

In Table 21, the patterns of answers to the questions regarding the antecedents of self-leadership are summarized. As seen from the results, autonomy takes the lead as it was expressed in answers for every question. Feeling trusted and recognized were stated to be both a facilitator and a blocker in terms of self-leadership. An effective managerial style was not identified as a facilitator in the interviews but it was identified as a blocker when lacking in addition to expectations that it would positively and negatively affect self-leadership skills. Competition increased the use of self-leadership skills when present and was quoted as a possible blocker when absent. Training opportunities led to decreased self-leadership when absent and was expected to be a possible facilitator when present. Perceptions of justice was usually handled from the negative side and expressed to hinder the use of self-leadership when lacking, and, as a consequence, it was also stated to be a possible blocker. In addition to that, it was also emphasized as a possible facilitator when the environment/practices were perceived to be just. Organizational culture/structure was not expressed as a normative effect but was stated to influence self-leadership hypothetically. Customer satisfaction was asserted to be a facilitator. An objective performance appraisal system was mentioned as being both a possible facilitator when present and a possible blocker when lacking. Promotion opportunities and clear career paths – identified as internal mobility – were expected to increase self-leadership, whereas task characteristics were asserted as a possible hinderer in terms of task routine. When the tasks were not challenging that could block the exertion of self-leadership skills. Clear job description was seen as another important factor due to the fact that it was expressed as an inhibitor when lacking, and was also regarded as a possible improver of self-leadership when present. Incentive rewards were also mentioned to facilitate the use of self-leadership skills.

Table 21: Summary of Common Patterns across Questions with regard to Frequencies

Factor	Facilitators in Current Organization (When Present)	Blockers in Current Organization (When Lacking)	Possible Facilitators (When Present)	Possible Blockers (When Lacking)	Total
Autonomy	7	2	3	5	17
Recognition	2	1		-	3
Feeling Trusted	2	?	-	-	4
Customer Satisfaction	2	-	-	-	2
Incentive Reward	3	-	-	-	3
Performance Appraisal	2	-	3	2	7
Internal Mobility	1	-	2	-	3

Factor	Facilitators in Current Organization (When Present)	Blockers in Current Organization (When Lacking)	Possible Facilitators (When Present)	Possible Blockers (When Lacking)	Total
Competition	2	1	-	1	4
Justice	-	3	4	1	8
Extensive Training	-	1	3	-	4
Clear Job Descriptions	-	1	1	-	2
Fair/Open Organizational Culture/Structure	-	-	3	4	7
Challenging Tasks	-	-	-	3	3
Effective Manager	-	3	3	5	11

In Table 22, facilitator and blockers were added up without differentiating whether they are actual or possible influences. This is done in order to see whether a factor is more repeated as a facilitator or a blocker. With regard to this reasoning, autonomy, recognition, customer satisfaction, HPWS dimension-incentive reward, performance appraisal, internal mobility and extensive training, and lateral organizational structures are expressed more as facilitators whereas an unfair organizational culture, routine tasks and an ineffective management were repeated more as blockers. Feeling trusted, competition, justice and job descriptions were repeated the same amount in these two categories. The possible explanations of these differences will be further evaluated in Chapter 5.

Table 22: Facilitators and Blockers of Self-Leadership (Combined Frequencies)

Factor	Facilitators (Combined)	Blockers (Combined)
Autonomy	10	7
Recognition	2	1
Feeling Trusted	2	2
Customer Satisfaction	2	-
Incentive Reward	3	-
Results-oriented Appraisal	5	2
Internal Mobility	3	-
Competition	2	2

Factor	Facilitators (Combined)	Blockers (Combined)
Justice	4	4
Extensive Training	3	1
Clear Job Descriptions	1	1
Fair/Open Organizational Culture/Structure	3	4
Challenging Tasks	-	3
Effective Manager	3	8

To sum up, the themes expressed during interviews are grouped under 4 categories: 1) Organizational system-related factors; 2) Leader/Manager-related factors; 3) Task characteristics; and 4) External factors. These groups represent the source of the factor that affects self-leadership. The grouping of the variables can be seen in Table 23.

Table 23: Sources of Factors Influencing Self-Leadership

Group (Source)	Factor	Frequency	Total Frequency
Organizational System Related Factors	Autonomy	17	58
	Recognition	3	
	Incentive Reward	3	
	Performance Appraisal	7	
	Internal Mobility	3	
	Extensive Training	4	
	Competition	4	
	Distributive Justice	8	
	Job Descriptions	2	
	Culture/Structure	7	
Leader/Manager-Related Factors	Effective Manager	11	15
	Feeling trusted	4	
Task Characteristics	Challenging Tasks	3	3
External Factors	Customer Satisfaction	2	2

As seen from the table, contextual factors have a great impact on self-leadership. This finding complements the results of Study 1 and expands new directions in terms of situational factors that can influence the use of self-leadership skills.

With regard to outcomes, increased performance/productivity, work engagement, self-confidence, self-development, and better stress and time management were expressed as factors that self-leadership contributed to. In line with Study 1, work engagement was expressed as an outcome, and in this respect, the results provide supporting evidence for Study 1 besides emphasizing the importance of self-leadership by clarifying other possible consequences. In Table 24, the outcomes expressed and their respective frequencies can be seen.

Table 24: Factors Influenced by Self-leadership

Factor	Frequency
Performance/Productivity	9
Self-development	3
Work Engagement	3
Self-confidence	2
Stress and Time Management	2

Chapter 5 Discussion and conclusion

Abstract: In this section, the findings acquired in this research are discussed and implications for theory and practice are presented. In this regard, first, the studies are briefly summarized and results are elaborated. Then, limitations are mentioned and conclusions are drawn.

5.1 Discussion

Self-leadership has emerged as a concept that is offered as a substitute for external leadership. It is based on the premises of self-regulation and asserts that when individuals are capable of directing and monitoring themselves, then they will require no external control or supervision. Many of the leadership theories have neglected the potential of the followers. Self-leadership, in this respect shifts the center of attention from the leader to the individual. Followers mean much more for organizations in current business world. Human resources have become the critical tool to gain a competitive edge and to survive. Realizing the potential of the followers and actualizing it have become crucial factors. In this respect, self-leadership has paved the way for a new approach in organizational context. Therefore, this research aims to identify some of the possible antecedents and outcomes of self-leadership in order to show how it can be facilitated and to emphasize its importance.

In this respect, two studies are conducted. The first one is a quantitative study to test two separate models. In these models, transformational leadership and high-performance work systems are investigated as contextual determinants whereas proactive personality is explored as a dispositional antecedent. As outcomes, work engagement and organizational citizenship behavior are analyzed, with a focus on the mediating effect of self-efficacy. Data is collected via survey method. In order to set the overarching theoretical framework for the hypotheses, self-determination theory is used. Self-determination theory (SDT) asserts that individuals have a tendency to be self-determining, to choose for themselves and to decide on their own will. Through SDT, people are able to satisfy their three basic needs: need for autonomy, need for relatedness and need for competence. In this respect, self-leadership is offered as a possible tool that can satisfy these basic needs.

In the second study, in-depth interviews are conducted to gain a deeper insight about the contextual antecedents and consequences of self-leadership, and to open up fields for future research directions.

First, we will elaborate on the results of the hypothesized relationships in Study 1. All hypotheses except H8 were fully supported whereas H8 was partially supported. The first three hypotheses were based on Model 1, which proposed positive relationships between anticipated determinants and self-leadership.

H1 hypothesized that, as a contextual determinant, transformational leadership would make a positive contribution to self-leadership; as the leader performed higher transformational leadership characteristics, the followers would be more inclined to exert self-leadership strategies. Results show that this hypothesis is supported. In a way, it means that a transformational leader can have the capacity to transform the individuals to self-leaders. With the help of the vision the leader creates, he/she can encourage the followers to take initiative and determine their own goals. This result has provided evidence that transformational leadership style has a direct effect on the exertion of self-leadership skills.

Although the research mainly concentrates on the ways to turn individuals to self-leaders, the necessity of a designated leader cannot be ignored in organizations. Pearce and Manz (2005) state that even in organizations that practice empowerment and delegation, there are designated leaders as a requirement within the organizational structure. The role of the leaders is to provide a role model for the followers and to teach them to direct themselves. From a social learning perspective, the followers may imitate the behavior of the leader and finally can have the capacity to replace him. In this respect, until self-managing teams emerge and are able to lead themselves, the role of the leader cannot be neglected.

H2 hypothesized that implementation of high-performance work systems would positively contribute to the exertion of self-leadership strategies. Results show that this expectation is also met. When the organizations use high-performance work systems, then the employees are more likely to lead themselves. This includes factors such as extensive training, internal mobility, employment security, clear job descriptions, results-oriented appraisal, incentive rewards and participation. Which factor contributes mostly to the development of self-leadership skills could not be identified since the construct yielded a one-factor structure. The results of Study 2 have given hints to answer this question. This will be discussed while evaluating the results of Study 2.

When comparing the two conceptual antecedents of self-leadership, the results show that transformational leadership is less effective than high-performance work systems. In literature, there are studies showing the greater effect of organizational level variables on work outcomes compared to leader's influence. In a recent study conducted by Pongpearchan (2016), it was seen that both transformational leadership and HPWS positively contributed to job motivation. The results showed that the effect of transformational leadership was slightly less with a Beta of 0.611 compared to HPWS which yielded a Beta of 0.678. In another study done by Oliveira and Silva (2015), the effects of HPWS and leader-member exchange on employee engagement were investigated. The regression results confirmed positive relationships between these variables. HPWS were able to explain 28% of the variance in employee engagement whereas leader-member exchange quality increased this ratio by a further 5%. As these results suggest, the presence of organizational level practices contribute more to positive individual level outcomes when compared to leadership attributes. The leader's approach to the followers may be influential on these statistics. The followers' perception of leadership behavior is highly dependent on the quality of the dyadic relationship between the leader and themselves, whereas high-performance work systems imply a more general and objective framework as they are implemented by the organization at approximately the same level. As leader-member exchange theory suggests, leaders have an in-group and an out-group. In-group or inner circle represents the followers who have closer relationships with the leader and to whom the leaders pay more attention. In this respect, it can be claimed that all of the followers of a leader are not subject to equal treatment; therefore, the effect of these dyadic relationships can be considered as less influential and effective compared to organizational level variables. Within the framework of this research, this explanation is only applicable for transformational leadership. HPWS is found to be more effective than transformational leadership, but this cannot be generalized over all leadership styles. The key finding here is that situational factors have a direct influence over self-leadership.

H3 hypothesized a positive relationship between proactive personality and self-leadership. The results confirm that the more proactive a person is, the more self-leadership strategies he/she uses. In line with the findings, research suggests that leaders displaying proactive personality traits are more likely to take "self-initiated and future-focused leading actions that are persistently sustained to bring changes toward the environment" (Wu & Wang, 2011, p. 305). It means that proactive personality facilitates goal-oriented self action. Here, it is seen that not only leaders but also employees can pursue self leadership strategies when they are, by nature, proactive. Another important point to mention is that, proactive personality contributed to self-leadership more when compared to contextual antecedents. It shows us that, although self-leadership can be facilitated through external mechanisms, the effect of personality establishes the basic or most influential driver to exert these skills.

H4 claimed that self-leadership would positively contribute to work engagement. This hypothesis is also supported. Work engagement includes one's devotion to work physically, cognitively and emotionally. In this respect, when one is able to lead himself/herself and establish personal goals, he/she will be more devoted to achieve these goals. Britt and colleagues claim that when the individual feels he/she has control over his/her job (autonomy) and performance is important, engagement will be high (Britt, Dickinson, Greene, & McKibben, 2007). A strong sense of self-control and self-efficacy are also stated to be facilitators of work engagement (Tuckey, Bakker, & Dollard, 2012). This increased sense of self-worth and self-influence acts as psychological capital for work engagement (Bakker & Leiter, 2010; Xanthopoulou et al., 2007). Therefore, a self-leading individual who has set personal goals, who can direct himself/herself and who tracks his/her own development is expected to engage more in work.

In accordance with H5, a positive relationship between self-leadership and organizational citizenship behavior is also found. The scale used for examination was not able to identify the difference between OCB-O and OCB-I; therefore, OCB is treated as a general construct. In literature, OCB is evaluated as contextual performance to distinguish it from task performance. In this respect, OCB is generally treated as a part of performance that goes beyond task requirements and emphasizes an altruistic approach. Previous research provides examples of studies proving a positive relationship between self-leadership and work role performance (e.g., Hauschildt & Konradt, 2012; Prussia et al., 1998). In line with this, OCB is also positively affected from self-leadership. With a similar rationale to work engagement, a person who values performance and self-development is likely to try preserving organizational well-being at all levels including colleagues.

Parallel to previous research, the sixth hypothesis regarding the relationship between self-leadership and self-efficacy is also supported. Self-leadership and self-efficacy are rooted in similar theoretical bases, and, therefore, move generally in the same direction. When employees set goals for themselves and act accordingly, they have the opportunity to evaluate themselves. When they are able to meet envisioned standards, it helps to increase their self-efficacy levels.

The last two hypotheses questioned the mediating role of self-efficacy between the independent variable self-leadership and the dependent variables work engagement and organizational citizenship behavior. The results showed that self-efficacy fully mediated the relationship between work engagement and self-leadership whereas the hypothesis regarding organizational citizenship behavior was only partially supported. The mediator is regarded as the psychological process that results in behaviors (Viney & King, 1998). In models that investigate intervening variables, it is generally hard to see full mediation due to the fact that many psychological processes may take part in explaining the relationship. In H7, full mediation is observed. It means that, self-leadership contributes to work engagement via increasing self-efficacy beliefs of the employees. But in H8, this effect is only partially supported. This can be the result of the altruistic nature of organizational citizenship behavior. Self-efficacy is a self-oriented concept, and, therefore, can effect work engagement which is again related with the self. On the other hand, organizational citizenship goes beyond the concerns of oneself and requires dedication of one's resources to all, not solely to the self for self-oriented goals. In this respect, self-efficacy, in a way, fails to meet the prerequisites of organizational citizenship behavior when compared to other possible altruistic mediators.

The second study is conducted by in-depth interview method to see if the findings complement the results in Study 1 and to investigate other possible determinants and outcomes of self-leadership more deeply. The results regarding the antecedents are categorized under four headings: facilitators in current organization, blockers in current organization, possible facilitators and possible blockers. Afterwards, the answers were transcribed and classified under relevant concepts. The themes that emerged during the analyses were autonomy, managerial style, organizational culture/structure, justice, recognition, competition, task characteristics, and some HPWS dimensions- performance appraisal, extensive training, incentive reward, internal mobility and job descriptions. These themes were grouped under four categories: organizational system-related factors, manager-/leader-related factors, task characteristics and external factors. The mostly repeated items were related to the systemic practices offered by the organization. It provided support for the argument that contextual factors were effective in facilitating and hindering the use of self-leadership skills.

The results showed that the mostly repeated factor in facilitating self-leadership was autonomy. Interviewees mentioned that they should not be interrupted and should take initiative in order to exert self-leadership skills. They asserted that, otherwise, close supervision would affect them negatively. This is not surprising as autonomy can be treated as a prerequisite for exerting self-leadership. Different from participation, autonomy is based on personal space. In autonomy, one can decide on his own and take initiative whereas, in participation, someone is included into something going on. Park and colleagues (2016) state that people put out more effort in contexts that support autonomy and competence. Autonomy is treated as a job resource (Demerouti et al., 2001). It means that, in order for the individual to experience positive outcomes, the required resources should be given. In our framework, autonomy is the basic resource of self-leadership. From a self-determination perspective, the need for autonomy should be satisfied for an individual to be able to lead himself/herself. The organization should provide an autonomous atmosphere for the individual to exert more self-leadership skills.

The second mostly emphasized factor in determining self-leadership was managerial style. Interviewees mentioned that bad/unsuccessful/strict managers hindered their self-leadership skills. Manager capabilities were expressed mostly as a blocker. It means that an ineffective manager can hinder the use of self-leadership more than an effective manager can facilitate. This corresponds with the results of Study 1. As seen from the analyses, transformational leadership contributed to self-leadership positively. But this contribution is less than the contribution of HPWS and proactive personality. It means that system-related factors such as high-performance work practices are more effective in facilitating self-leadership when compared to dyadic factors and that the effect of contextual factors on self-leadership is again exemplified.

In line with that, another variable that serves as a blocker of self-leadership in its absence and as a facilitator when present was a fair and open organizational culture. As the interviewees mention, when the culture is bureaucratic and is not open to new ideas, their self-leadership skills will be blocked. Previous research shows that an empowering, open climate and autonomy positively affect the use of self-leadership at team level (e.g., Seibert, Silver, & Randolph, 2004). In this respect, it can be claimed that in order for self-leadership to emerge and develop, a culture that values innovation, creativity and achievement is required. As the interviewees state, classical approaches and bureaucratic organizations do not help them to use self-leadership skills. When the culture is not convenient, self-leadership cannot be born and raised. Also, lateral organizational structures are implied to facilitate self-leadership. An interviewee mentioned that in lateral structures self-leadership would flourish more easily. It means that when the organization is horizontal, information flows more fluently and communication is better. People can transfer their knowledge and skills to each other more easily. In this respect, culture and structure are effective in determining the use of self-leadership. In order to enhance it, an open organizational culture and a lateral structure that eases the settlement of this culture can be helpful.

Justice was another factor that was mentioned regularly during the interviews. It has been asserted as both a facilitator and a blocker in its absence. As equity theory suggests, individuals long for fairness when they compare their input/output ratio to those of others who exert the same effort (Adams, 1965). Park et al. (2016) show that self-leadership acts as a partial mediator in the relationship between organizational justice and work engagement. This proves us that organizational justice contributes significantly to self-leadership. When individuals feel that they are treated equally and fairly, their intrinsic motivation increases and they tend to put up effort to exert self-leadership. In the contrary case, they feel that their efforts are meaningless and do not affect the outcome. Therefore, they tend to decrease their efforts to achieve better. Also, considered from a social exchange perspective, people are inclined to perform better when they believe that their efforts will yield the results they expect. Therefore, the level of self-leadership can be dependent on how fair the individuals perceive the work environment to be.

In line with that, trust among employees is stated to bear intrinsic motivation (Tyler & Blader, 2000). As expressed by some interviewees, feeling trusted is another factor that contributes to self-leadership and hinders it when lacking. Trust helps to satisfy the needs for relatedness and autonomy. It means that when the employees feel that their managers trust them, they feel both included and empowered. The pattern across the answers shows that the employees do not want to let down their managers. They want to compensate for the initiative given to them. This is logical both from the social exchange perspective and self-determination perspective. They try to perform better via using self-leadership strategies in order to reciprocate the trust that their leader has shown towards them and they also have the autonomy to do their job via this trust. Therefore, the need for autonomy is also satisfied.

Recognition can also be considered as a part of that relationship. Interviewees imply that they want their efforts to be recognized and appreciated. The system should be visible so that their supervisors can see and judge their abilities. When their managers or colleagues see what they achieve, they become more willing to put out effort through increased intrinsic motivation.

As indicated by some interviewees, customer satisfaction is another factor that leads the individuals to use self leadership strategies more. The logic is parallel to recognition, but customer satisfaction is different in that it is an outside source. It is not a part of the system or the organization. When the customers are happy with the outcome of the transaction between themselves and the employees, this feedback enhances the intrinsic motivation of the employees to maintain and develop their performance. This factor differentiates it from the others in that customer satisfaction is an external factor and comes from the outside after the transaction is complete. Therefore, this finding is especially important and shows us that not only internal factors but also external factors can affect the level of self-leadership exerted by the employees.

Competition was stated to be another facilitator and hinderer of self-leadership. Self-leadership, in fact, is proposed as a solution to the increasing competition within the business environment. Therefore, it shows us that this proposition, in a way, justifies itself. When competition is high, people tend to exert more self-leadership skills. Competition is regarded as a part of intrinsic motivation (Csikszentmihalyi, 1975) and achievement motivation (McClelland, Atkinson, Clark, & Lowell, 1953). When competition is low, people see no reason to exert more effort and to motivate themselves to aim for better. In this respect, a competitive organizational environment can act as a tool to facilitate self-leadership skills.

Task characteristics have the same logic. Interviewees implied that routine and non-challenging tasks would hinder their self-leadership skills. In routine tasks, they cannot find the satisfaction they long for and their basic needs are not fulfilled. Langfred (2005) showed that team level self-leadership was more effective when the team engaged in more complex tasks. In this respect, it can be concluded that in the absence of tasks requiring creativity, an individual would be less inclined to exert self-leadership. This finding is also important because it adds another dimension to the previous results obtained in Study 1. In both studies, system-related factors and leadership style emerged as the main antecedents of self-leadership. With Study 2, the effect of task characteristics is also exemplified and this has revealed another dimension that can directly influence self-leadership.

Lastly, the results corresponding to the dimensions of HPWS will be elaborated. Results-oriented performance appraisal, incentive reward, internal mobility, extensive training and clear job descriptions were stated as some factors that could flourish or hinder self-leadership.

Performance appraisal was the most repeated factor among all and was expressed mostly as a facilitator. Establishment of an objective and measurable performance system that emphasizes the achievement of long-term goals is expressed to contribute to self-leadership development. These kind of systems enable the employees to track their performance and see their weaknesses and strengths. In this respect, they serve as supporters to control and regulate behavior. Therefore, in an organization with established performance standards, employees may perceive it easier to evaluate their improvement. They know how they will be evaluated and can see clearly what is expected from them. Consequently, they are able to regulate their behavior; these systems help them to revise and alter their own goals accordingly.

Second comes extensive training. Interviewees mentioned the existence of training and development opportunities to be mostly a facilitator. Without training, one cannot be expected to go beyond his/her own limits and increase their performance. Previous research also shows that training has positively contributed to the use of self-leadership strategies (e.g., Frayne & Latham, 1987; Latham & Frayne, 1989; Neck & Manz, 1996). With these activities, one can feel more competent over his/her job and track his/her performance better.

After training, incentive reward was expressed to be a facilitator. Together with justice perceptions, rewards are also treated as a part of social transaction. In this respect, individuals want to see that their efforts are fairly evaluated and rewarded; therefore, incentive reward guarantees that their wages/bonuses will be based on their actual performance. So, when they are paid for their performance, it enables the individuals to develop a sense of control over their work, satisfying needs for autonomy (Lawler, Mohrman, & Ledford, 1992). Ignoring all other factors, monetary gain is, by itself, a major motivator to perform better. Therein, when the subject is rewards, it's not surprising to expect individuals to aim for better than they have previously done.

Another factor matching up with HPWS dimensions was internal mobility. The interviewees mentioned that promotion opportunities and clear career paths facilitated their self-leadership. If one sees a future for himself/herself within the organization, then he/she is expected to exert more self-leadership skills. This is very similar to the reasoning behind the results-oriented appraisal dimension. If they sense that they have the probability to get a higher position and/or wage, then they are likely to regulate themselves in order to reach the required performance level.

Last factor that the interviewees expressed was clear job descriptions. In order to regulate behavior, one would need a clear, established job description that will show him the boundaries and responsibilities of his/her job. This may help the individual to develop a sense of control over his/her task area, become more competent within those limits and set goals for himself/herself more easily. Therefore, clarifying ambiguity in terms of job can enhance the development of self-leadership skills.

When the overall picture in terms of the antecedents of self-leadership is taken into consideration, the most striking result is that system-related contextual factors are the most effective ones among all. Study 1 has shown us that HPWS has a direct effect on self-leadership and Study 2 has provided evidence for the fact that especially some dimensions of HPWS – performance appraisal, reward systems, internal mobility, job descriptions and training – influence the exertion of self-leadership skills. When these results are elaborated together, organizational system-related factors emerge as the most influential antecedents of self-leadership within the framework of this research. This effect is followed by the contribution of leadership style. Study 1 has provided support for the direct effect of transformational leadership on self-leadership. Complementing that, Study 2 has shown that an open, empowering leader can facilitate self-leadership whereas a strict leader can block or hinder the use of these skills. This shows us that effective managerial style is another important factor that directly affects the level of self-leadership.

The last part of Study 2 concentrated on the outcomes of self-leadership. Interviewees were asked to tell what contribution the use of self-leadership strategies makes to them. The statements showed that performance, self-confidence, self-development, work engagement and stress/time management were affected by self-leadership.

Performance/productivity was the mostly mentioned factor among all. Previous research is supportive of this finding and shows that there is a positive relationship between self-leadership and performance (e.g., Frayne & Geringer, 2000; Konradt et al., 2009; Neck & Manz, 1996; Prussia et al., 1998; Uhl-Bien & Graen, 1998). As the interviewees propose, setting goals and establishing performance standards expedite actually reaching that performance. Success was also expressed during the interviews. This was exemplified by a study conducted by Murphy and Ensher (2001). They showed that individuals who established their own goals and who used self-management strategies, reported higher levels of perceived career success.

In line with the results of Study 1, self-leadership was indicated as a contributor to work engagement in the interviews. The participants stated that with the help of self-leadership strategies, they enjoyed their work and took pleasure. As discussed before, the sense of self-control over the outcomes may be effective in increasing the joy and enthusiasm the employee experiences.

Self-confidence was also expressed to be another outcome. Similar to self-efficacy, self-confidence or esteem may act as a catalyzer between self-leadership and other job outcomes. Stajkovic and Luthans (1998) claim that when individuals lead themselves, they are likely to be more confident, and through that confidence, more successful. The exertion of power and control over own goals, self-punishment and self-rewards, and being in charge serve as factors that can increase self-confidence.

In a similar fashion, people who engage in self-leadership strategies, tend to feel themselves improved. Individuals exerting self-leadership can determine their needs and wants, adapt themselves accordingly and go for the extra mile. Therefore, self-leadership contributes to self-development.

Last outcome mentioned in the interviews was the ability to manage stress and time. Saks and Ashforth (1997) suggest that having control is associated with lower stress and anxiety. Therefore, it is very likely that self-leading individuals are better at coping with stress. In a similar way, these individuals can determine their own schedules and plan their own time tables as they regulate themselves. Thus, self-leadership can enhance individuals' time management skills.

5.2 Implications

Self-leadership has become an important concept in order for organizations to cope with the volatility of the business world. Employees should learn to regulate their own behavior without needing the supervision of an external leader, or the role of the leader should only be coaching or mentoring. A close supervision culture, usually, fails to meet the requirements of current business environment. Two major factors lie behind this. First of all, some individuals value autonomy, they are qualified and do not accept being directed. Second factor is the competition. When the organizations rely on bureaucratic procedures and adopt a control culture, sometimes, they cannot respond and change quickly. Therefore, rather than attributing great power to someone, distribution of power is required. In this respect, self-leadership offers a potential to be utilized.

As discussed previously, this research examined some determinants and consequences of self-leadership. Besides providing an organizational survival advantage, at the individual level, self-leadership contributes to important outcomes such as performance, work engagement and organizational citizenship behavior. Therefore, supporting the development of these skills may enhance these positive consequences, which in return, will also benefit the organization.

As seen from the results, some macro variables such as managerial approach and organizational culture play an important role in determining self-leadership. Especially in terms of leadership, organizations should thrive for a fair, open, sensible manager/leader who communicates with the employees effectively and cares for their improvement. Therefore, an organizational culture that is supportive of this should also be adopted. People want to work in organizations that are open to new ideas, innovation and change.

Another important implication can be drawn for human resources departments. Study 1 has shown that high-performance work systems play an

important role in facilitating self-leadership. Study 2 has also provided supporting evidence for this and has indicated that especially HPWS dimensions regarding performance appraisal, training, reward systems and internal mobility are
effective in determining the level of self-leadership. As seen from both studies,
people value fair treatment, objective performance appraisal, career opportunities and training. Human resources departments should be aware of that and
donate the people with the trainings they require or wish for. They should set-
tle an open performance appraisal system in which everyone can follow their
development and get feedback from colleagues. The employees' responsibilities
should be clear and they should only be responsible for what they are capable to
do. It may be hard to achieve as circumstances change, but, during recruitment,
human resources practitioners may take these into account to match the right
person with the right job.

As the answers suggest, people do not like uncertainty. They want to clearly
see where they can be in the future, how much they will be paid for something
and how they will be evaluated. Therefore, openness should be embraced in every level and every practice of the organization.

5.3 Future research directions

There are some gaps in the study that can further be investigated. First of all,
although the industrial differences are investigated, this research lacks in identi-
fying whether a variation occurs between public and private sectors in terms of
self-leadership. Intuitively, it can be claimed that private organizations may donate the employees with greater autonomy compared to public organizations due
to the fact that public sector is dominated with more strict rules and practices.

Another important point to mention is that, the results of Study 2 have implied a broad range of candidate variables that can facilitate or hinder the development of self-leadership. Though some of these variables were investigated in
Study 1, the others such as competition, trust, task characteristics, etc. can be
regarded as possible antecedents of self-leadership. Also, in addition to engagement, other outcomes such as performance, self-development, self-confidence,
stress and time management were expressed as consequences of self-leadership.
In this respect, Study 2 has paved the way for future research over these variables.

The effect of culture is another subject of question. To exemplify, in cultures
where power-distance is high, it's hard to constitute a self-leadership climate.
The rough hierarchical levels can hinder information flow, weaken initiative opportunities and impair employees' self-confidence.

Another possible question that arises from the findings is about the mediator role of self-efficacy between self-leadership and organizational citizenship behavior. As the results suggest, the hypothesis is only partially supported. Therefore, other variables may be investigated to see whether a better explanation can be drawn. For example, Plessis and Barkhuizen (2011) state that in order to create a caring environment in organizations, psychological capital is a prerequisite. In a recent study conducted by Qadeer and Jaffery (2014), it was found that psychological capital mediated the relationship between organizational climate and organizational citizenship behavior towards both the organization and colleagues. Self-leadership may enhance the psychological resources of an individual. Therefore, psychological capital may be a candidate to mediate the relationship between self-leadership and organizational citizenship behavior.

5.4 Limitations

There are some points that we have to mention when considering the results. First of all, the research is cross-sectional, and, therefore, the relationships among the variables reflect a definite point in time. In this respect, longitudinal methods can be applied to see how the variables change over time.

Data is collected from firms operating in Istanbul and the generalizability of the results is subject to question. Although Istanbul is a metropolitan city and can be treated as reflecting the major demographical characteristic of Turkey, the findings are dependent on the sample and research is needed to be repeated over different samples.

In terms of the second study, the sample size is a major limitation. The interviews can be conducted in larger samples to see if a pattern emerges. Although candidate variables are established for future research, which one is more likely to have the major effect cannot be identified due to low sample size.

Another limitation with regard to the second study is that the distribution of the sample in terms of industry does not match with the distribution in Study 1. Although the findings of both studies complement and provide support for each other, the difference between the sample distributions should be taken into account and the results should be approached cautiously.

A last point to mention is that the theoretical framework assumes that people are inclined to be self-determined. Although autonomy is considered as a basic need, some people may not have the opportunity to fulfill this need. In contexts that do not offer high recognition or trust, employees may not find space to exert self-leadership and self-leading behaviors may not be reinforced. Also, as Williams (1997) suggests, there is an absorptive capacity of every individual;

therefore, it cannot be expected that interventions in context will yield in same outcomes for every single employee. Learning is based on the previous knowledge and capability of the worker and the extent of contribution that will be brought about by the changes in the context, can be dependent on the characteristics of the employee.

5.5 Conclusions

Self-leadership is a set of strategies that enable an individual to regulate his behavior and cognitions in order to reach pre-established goals. It has become a crucial concept for organizations as the competition increases and the dynamics of business environment change. In this respect, this research aims to determine some possible antecedents and consequences of self-leadership.

Besides its vitality for organizations, self-leadership is seen to have essential effects on individual level outcomes such as work engagement, performance and OCB. This research provides corroborative support for the importance of self-leadership.

Transformational leadership, HPWS and proactive personality were investigated as the possible antecedents at the first study. They all were found to contribute to self-leadership. Literature on self-leadership is generally based on the relationships between dispositional factors and self-leadership. In this regard, this research shows that contextual factors such as leadership style and HPWS can also contribute to the exertion of self-leadership strategies. The results of the second study also confirm this and also show that task characteristics and some external factors such as customer satisfaction are also effective in determining the level of self-leadership.

Although dispositional factors such as proactive personality have a great effect on the emergence of self-leadership, it is conceptualized as a learned behavior rather than a trait and it is a different concept than personality (Manz, 1986; Stewart, Carson & Cardy, 1996). Therefore, self-leadership can be enhanced through contextual mechanisms and this research provides an example for that proposition.

References

Adams, J. S. (1965). Inequity in social exchange. In L. Berkowitz (Ed.), *Advances in experimental social psychology* (pp. 267–299). New York: Academic Press.

Amabile, T. M., Hill, K. G., Hennessey, B. A., & Tighe, E. M. (1994). The work preference inventory: Assessing intrinsic and extrinsic motivational orientations. *Journal of Personality and Social Psychology, 66*(November), 950–967.

Andressen, P., Konradt, U., & Neck, P. C. (2012). The relation between self-leadership and transformational leadership: Competing models and the moderating role of virtuality. *Journal of Leadership & Organizational Studies, 19*(1), 68–82.

Arthur, J. B. (1994). Effects of human resource systems on manufacturing performance and turnover. *Academy of Management Journal, 37*(3), 670–687.

Avolio, B. J., & Bass, B. M. (1995). You can drag a horse to water, but you can't make it drink, except when it is thirsty. *Journal of Leadership Studies, 5,* 1–17.

Avolio, B. J., & Bass, B. M. (2002). *Developing potential across a full range of leadership.* Mahwah, NJ: Lawrence Erlbaum Associates.

Avolio, B. J., & Gibbons, T. C. (1988). Developing transformational leaders: A lifespan approach. In J. A. Conger & R. N. Kanungo (Eds.), *Charismatic leadership: The elusive factor in organizational effectiveness* (pp. 276–308). San Francisco, CA: Jossey-Bass.

Bakker, A. B., & Leiter, M. P. (Eds.). (2010). *Work engagement: A handbook of essential theory and research.* New York: Psychology Press.

Bamberger, P., & Meshoulam, I. (2000). *Human resource strategy.* Thousand Oaks, CA: Sage.

Bandura, A. (1977). *Social learning theory.* Englewood Cliffs, NJ: Prentice-Hall.

Bandura, A. (1994). Self-efficacy. In V. S. Ramachaudran (Ed.), *Encyclopedia of human behavior* (pp. 71–81). New York: Academic Press. (Reprinted in H. Friedman (Ed.), *Encyclopedia of mental health.* San Diego, CA: Academic Press, 1998).

Bandura, A. (1997). *Self-efficacy: The exercise of control.* New York: W. H. Freeman.

Bandura, A., & Cervone, D. (1983). Self-evaluative and self-efficacy mechanisms governing the motivational effects of goal systems. *Journal of Personality and Social Psychology, 45*(5), 1017–1028.

Baron, R. M., & Kenny, D. A. (1986). The moderator-mediator variable distinction in social psychological research: Conceptual, strategic, and statistical considerations. *Journal of Personality and Social Psychology*, *51*(6), 1173–1182.

Bass, B. M. (1998). *Transformational leadership: Industrial, military, and educational impact*. Mahwah, NJ: Lawrence Erlbaum Associates.

Bass, B. M., & Avolio, B. J. (1990). The implications of transactional and transformational leadership for individual, team, and organizational development. In R. W. Woodman & W. A. Pasmore (Eds.), *Research in organizational change and development* (pp. 231–272). Greenwich, CT: JAI Press.

Bass, B. M., & Avolio, B. J. (1995). *The multifactor leadership questionnaire*. Palo Alto, CA: Mind Garden.

Bateman, T. S., & Crant, J. M. (1993). The proactive component of organizational behavior. *Journal of Organizational Behavior*, *14*(2), 103–118.

Batt, R., & Applebaum, E. (1995). Worker participation in diverse settings: Does the form affect the outcome, and if so, who benefits? *British Journal of Industrial Relations*, *33*(3), 353–378.

Beauregard, T. A. (2012). Perfectionism, self-efficacy and OCB: The moderating role of gender. *Personnel Review*, *41*(5), 590–608.

Becherer, R. C., & Maurer, J. G. (1999). The proactive personality disposition and entrepreneurial behavior among small company presidents. *Journal of Small Business Management*, *38*(1), 28–36.

Becker, B. E., & Huselid, M. A. (1998). High performance work systems and firm performance: A synthesis of research and managerial implications. In G. R. Ferris (Ed.), *Research in personnel and human resources management* (pp. 53–101). Stamford, CT: JAI Press.

Bindl, U., & Parker, S. (2011). Proactive work behavior: Forward-thinking and change-oriented action in organizations. In S. Zedeck (Ed.), *APA handbook of industrial and organizational psychology* (pp. 567–598). Washington, DC: American Psychological Association.

Birdi, K., Clegg, C., Patterson, M., Robinson, A., Stride, C. B., Wall, T. D., & Wood, S. J. (2008). The impact of human resources and operational management practices on company productivity: A longitudinal study. *Personnel Psychology*, *61*(3), 467–501.

Bozkurt, S., Ertemsir, E., & Bal, Y. (2014). A study evaluating the validity and reliability of high performance work systems (HPWS) scale in Turkish, *Proceedings of 12th International Academic Conference*, (pp. 187–195). Prague, Czech Republic: International Institute of Social and Economic Science.

Britt, T. W., Dickinson, J. M., Greene, T. M., & McKibben, E. S. (2007). Self-engagement at work. In C. L. Cooper & D. Nelson (Eds.), *Positive organizational behavior* (pp. 143–158). Thousand Oaks, CA: Sage Publications.

Bycio, P., Hackett, R. D., & Allen, J. S. (1995). Further assessments of Bass' conceptualization of transactional and transformational leadership. *Journal of Applied Psychology, 80*(4), 468–478.

Callahan, J. S., Brownlee, A. L., Brtek, M. D., & Tosi, H. L. (2003). Examining the unique effects of multiple motivational sources on task performance. *Journal of Applied Social Psychology, 33*(1), 2515–2535.

Cameron, R. (2009). A sequential mixed model research design: Design, analytical and display issues. *International Journal of Multiple Research Approaches, 3*(2), 140–152.

Carmeli, A., Meitar, R., & Weisberg, J. (2006). Self-leadership skills and innovative behavior at work. *International Journal of Manpower, 27*(1), 75–90.

Catley, D., & Duda, J. L. (1997). Psychological antecedents of the frequency and intensity of flow in golfers. *International Journal of Sports Psychology, 28*(4), 309–322.

Cerasoli, C. P., & Ford, M. T. (2014). Intrinsic motivation, performance, and the mediating role of mastery goal orientation: A test of self-determination theory. *The Journal of Psychology, 148*(3), 267–286.

Chadwick, C. (2010). Theoretic insights on the nature of performance synergies in human resource systems: Toward greater precision. *Human Resource Management Review, 20*(2), 85–101.

Chalofsky, N., & Krishna, V. (2009). Meaningfulness, commitment, and engagement: The intersection of a deeper level of intrinsic motivation. *Advances in Developing Human Resources, 11*(2), 189–203.

Chen, G., Gully, S. M., & Eden, D. (2004). General self-efficacy and self-esteem: Toward theoretical and empirical distinction between correlated self-evaluations. *Journal of Organizational Behavior, 25*(3), 375–395.

Cortina, J. M. (1993). What is coefficient alpha? An examination of theory and applications. *Journal of Applied Psychology, 78*(1), 98–104.

Crant, J. M. (1995). The proactive personality scale and objective job performance among real estate agents. *Journal of Applied Psychology, 80*(4), 532–537.

Crant, J. M. (2000). Proactive behavior in organizations. *Journal of Management, 26*(3), 435–462.

Crant, J. M., & Bateman, T. S. (2000). Charismatic leadership viewed from above: The impact of proactive personality. *Journal of Organizational Behavior, 21*(1), 63–75.

Csikszentmihalyi, M. (1975). *Beyond boredom and anxiety.* San Francisco, CA: Jossey-Bass.

Datta, D. K., Guthrie, J. P., & Wright, P. M. (2005). Human resource management and labor productivity: Does industry matter? *Academy of Management Journal, 48*(1), 135–145.

Deci, E. L., & Ryan, R. M. (1985). *Intrinsic motivation and self-determination in human behavior.* New York: Plenum Press.

Deci, E. L., & Ryan, R. M. (1987). The support of autonomy and the control of behavior. *Journal of Personality and Social Psychology, 53*(6), 1024–1037.

Deci, E. L., Ryan, R. M., Gagné, M., Leone, D. R., Usunov, J., & Kornazheva, B. P. (2001). Need satisfaction, motivation, and well-being in the work organizations of a former Eastern Bloc country. *Personality and Social Psychology Bulletin, 27*(8), 930–942.

Deci, E. L., Vallerand, R. J., Pelletier, L. G., & Ryan, M. R. (1991). Motivation and education: The self-determination perspective. *Educational Psychologist, 26*(3&4), 325–346.

Delery, J. E., & Doty, D. H. (1996). Modes of theorizing in strategic human resource management: Tests of universalistic, contingency, and configurational performance predictions. *Academy of Management Journal, 39*(4), 802–835.

Demerouti, E., Bakker, A. B., Nachreiner, F., & Schaufeli, W. B. (2001). The job demand resources model of burnout. *Journal of Applied Psychology, 86*(3), 499–512.

DiIorio, C., Faherty, B., & Manteuffel, B. (1992). The relationship of self-efficacy and social support in self-management of epilepsy. *Western Journal of Nursing Research, 14*(3), 292–303.

Dionne, S. D., Yammarino, F. J., Atwater, L. E., & Spangler, W. D. (2004). Transformational leadership and team performance. *Journal of Organizational Change Management, 17*(2), 177–193.

Dubrin, A. J. (2013). *Proactive personality and behavior for individual and organizational productivity.* Cheltenham, UK: Edward Elgar Publishing.

Dvir, T., Eden, D., Avolio, B. J., & Shamir, B. (2002). Impact of transformational leadership on follower development and performance: A field experiment. *Academy of Management Journal, 45*(4), 735–744.

Finkelstein, M. A. (2011). Intrinsic and extrinsic motivation and organizational citizenship behavior: A functional approach to organizational citizenship behavior. *Journal of Psychological Issues in Organizational Culture, 2*(1), 19–34.

Fornell, C., & Larcker, D. F. (1981). Evaluating structural equation models with unobservable variables and measurement error. *Journal of Marketing Research, 18*(1), 39–50.

Frayne, C. A., & Geringer, J. M. (2000). Self-management training for improving job performance: A field experiment involving salespeople. *Journal of Applied Psychology, 85*(3), 361–372.

Frayne, C. A., & Latham, G. P. (1987). Application of social-learning theory to employee self-management of attendance. *Journal of Applied Psychology, 72*(3), 387–392.

Frese, M., & Fay, D. (2001). Personal initiative: An active performance concept for work in the 21st century. In B. M. Staw & R. M. Sutton (Eds.), *Research in organizational behavior* (pp. 133–187). Amsterdam, the Netherlands: Elsevier Science.

Furtner, M. R., & Baldegger, U. (2013). *Self-leadership und Führung: Theorien, Modelle und praktische Umsetzung.* Wiesbaden, Germany: Springer Gabler Verlag.

Furtner, M. R., & Rauthmann, J. F. (2010). Relations between self-leadership and scores on the Big Five. *Psychological Reports, 107*(2), 339–353.

Furtner, M. R., Rauthmann, J. F., & Sachse, P. (2011). The self-loving self-leader: Examining relations between self-leadership and the Dark Triad. *Social Behavior and Personality, 39*(3), 369–380.

Gagné, M., & Deci, E. L. (2005). Self-determination theory and work motivation. *Journal of Organizational Behavior, 26*(4), 331–362.

Ganesan S., & Weitz B. A. (1996). The impact of staffing policies on retail buyer job attitudes and behavior. *Journal of Retailing, 72*, 31–56.

Gerhardt, M., Ashenbaum, B., & Newman, W. R. (2009). Understanding the impact of proactive personality on job performance: The roles of tenure and self-management. *Journal of Leadership and Organizational Studies, 16*(1), 61–72.

Godwin, J. L., Neck, C. P., & Houghton, J. D. (1999). The impact of thought self-leadership on individual goal performance: A cognitive perspective. *The Journal of Management Development, 18*(2), 153–169.

Goldberg, L. R. (1990). An alternative "description of personality": The big-five factor structure. *Journal of Personality and Social Psychology, 59*(6), 1216–1229.

Guthrie, J. P. (2001). High-involvement work practices, turnover, and productivity: Evidence from New Zealand. *Academy of Management Journal, 44*(1), 180–190.

Hagger, M. S., & Chatzisarantis, N. L. D. (Eds.). (2007). *Intrinsic motivation and self-determination in exercise and sport.* Champaign, IL: Human Kinetics.

Hair, J. F., Black, W. C., Babin, B. J., & Anderson, R. E. (2010). *Multivariate data analysis* (7th ed.). Upper Saddle River, NJ: Prentice Hall.

Hamel, G., & Prahalad, C. K. (2002). *Competing for the future*. Bombay, India: Tata McGraw-Hill Education.

Hauschildt, K., & Konradt, U. (2012). Self-leadership and team members' work role performance. *Journal of Managerial Psychology*, 27(5), 497–517.

Houghton, J. D., Bonham, T. W., Neck, C. P., & Singh, K. (2004). The relationship between self-leadership and personality: A comparison of hierarchical factor structures. *Journal of Managerial Psychology*, 19(4), 427–441.

Houghton, J. D., Dawley, D., & DiLiello, T. C. (2012). The abbreviated self-leadership questionnaire (ASLQ): A more concise measure of self-leadership. *International Journal of Leadership Studies*, 7(2), 216–232.

Houghton, J. D., & Yoho, S. K. (2005). Toward a contingency model of leadership and psychological empowerment: When should self-leadership be encouraged?. *Journal of Leadership and Organizational Studies*, 11(4), 65–83.

Houkes, I., Janssen, P. P. M., de Jonge, J., & Nijhuis, F. J. N. (2001). Specific relationships between work characteristics and intrinsic work motivation, burnout and turnover intention: A multi-sample analysis. *European Journal of Work and Organizational Psychology*, 10(1), 1–23.

Hu, L. T., & Bentler, P. M. (1999). Cutoff criteria for fit indexes in covariance structure analysis: Conventional criteria versus new alternatives. *Structural Equation Modeling*, 6(1), 1–55.

Huselid, M. A. (1995). The impact of human resource management practices on turnover, productivity and corporate financial performance. *Academy of Management Journal*, 38(3), 635–672.

İşbaşı, J. Ö. (2000). *Çalışanın yöneticilere duydukları güvenin örgütsel adalete ilişkin algılamalarının örgütsel vatandaşlık davranışının oluşumundaki rolü: Bir turizm örgütünde uygulama* (Unpublished Master's Thesis). Antalya, Turkey: Akdeniz University.

Jung, D. I., Chow, C., & Wu, A. (2003). The role of transformational leadership in enhancing organizational innovation: Hypotheses and some preliminary findings. *Leadership Quarterly*, 14(4), 525–545.

Kahn, W. A. (1990). Psychological conditions of personal engagement and disengagement at work. *Academy of Management Journal*, 33(4), 692–724.

Kerr, S., & Jermier, J. M. (1978). Substitutes for leadership: Their meaning and measurement. *Organizational Behavior and Human Performance*, 22(3), 375–403.

Kerr, S., & Slocum, J. W., Jr. (1981). Controlling the performance of people in organization. In W. Starbuck & İ. P. Nystrom (Eds.), *Handbook of organizations* (pp. 116–134). New York: Oxford University Press.

Kickul, J., & Gundry, L. K. (2002). Prospecting for strategic advantage: The proactive entrepreneurial personality and small firm innovation. *Journal of Small Business Management, 40*(2), 85–97.

Kim, J., Lee, I., Choi, B., Hong, S., Tam, K. Y., & Naruse, K. (2006). Toward reliable metrics for cultural aspects of human-computer interaction: Focusing on the mobile internet in three Asian countries. In D. Galetta & P. Zhang (Eds.), *Human-computer interaction and management information systems: Applications* (pp. 173–199). Armonk, NY: M. E. Sharpe.

Konradt, U., Andressen, P., & Ellwart, T. (2009). Self-leadership in organizational teams: A multilevel analysis of moderators and mediators. *European Journal of Work and Organizational Psychology, 18*(3), 322–346.

Langer, E. (1983). *The psychology of control.* Thousand Oaks, CA: Sage Publications.

Langfred, C. W. (2005). Autonomy and performance in teams: The multilevel moderating effect of task interdependence. *Journal of Management, 31*(4), 513–529.

Latham, G. P., & Frayne, C. A. (1989). Self-management training for increasing job attendance: A follow-up and a replication. *Journal of Applied Psychology, 74*(3), 411–416.

Lawler, E. E., Mohrman, S. A., & Ledford, G. E. (1992). *Creating high performance organizations.* San Francisco, CA: Jossey-Bass.

Lawler, E. E., & Rhode, J. G. (1976). *Information and control in organizations.* Pacific Palisades, CA: Goodyear.

Lee, H., Werner, S., & Kim, T. Y. (2016). High performance work systems and organization attraction: The moderating effects of vocational interests. *Employee Relations, 38*(5), 682–702.

Lee, J. W., & Bang, H. (2012). High performance work systems, person-organization fit and organizational outcomes. *Journal of Business Administration Research, 1*(2), 129–138.

Lee, M., & Koh, J. (2001). Is empowerment really a new concept? *International Journal of Human Resource Management, 12*(4), 684–695.

Leiter, M. P., & Maslach, C. (1988). The impact of interpersonal environment on burnout and organizational commitment. *Journal of Organizational Behavior, 9*(4), 297–308.

Leiter, M. P., & Maslach, C. (2004). Areas of work life: A structured approach to organizational predictors of job burnout. In P. Perrewé & C. D. Ganster (Eds.), *Research in occupational stress and well-being* (pp. 91–134). Oxford, England: JAI Press/Elsevier.

Lewis, P. V. (1996). *Transformational leadership: A new model for total church involvement*. Nashville, TN: Broadman & Holman.

Lin, Y. G., McKeachie, W. J., & Kim, Y. C. (2003). College student intrinsic and/or extrinsic motivation and learning. *Learning and Individual Differences, 13*(3), 251–258.

Locke, E. A., & Latham, G. P. (1990). *A theory of goal setting and task performance*. Englewood Cliffs, NJ: Prentice-Hall.

Maddux, J. E. (2002). Self-efficacy: The power of believing you can. In C. R. Snyder & S. J. Lopez (Eds.), *Handbook of positive psychology* (pp. 277–287). New York: Oxford University Press.

Mahoney, M. J., & Arnkoff, D. B. (1978). Cognitive and self-control therapies. In S. L. Garfield & A. E. Borgin (Eds.), *Handbook of psychotherapy and therapy change* (pp. 689–722). New York: Wiley.

Mahoney, M. J., & Arnkoff, D. B. (1979). Self-management: Theory, research, and application. In J. P. Brady & D. Pomerleau (Eds.), *Behavioral medicine: Theory and practice* (pp. 75–96). Baltimore, MD: Williams and Williams.

Mahoney, M. J., & Thoresen, C. E. (Eds.). (1974). *Self-control: Power to the person*. Monterey, CA: Brooks/Cole.

Manz, C. C. (1979). Sources of control: A behavior modification perspective. In Proceedings of the Eastern Academy of Management, pp. 82–88.

Manz, C. C. (1986). Self-leadership: Toward an expanded theory of self-influence processes in organizations. *Academy of Management Review, 11*(3), 585–600.

Manz, C. C. (1990). Beyond self-managing work teams: Toward self-leading teams in the workplace. In R. Woodman & W. Pasmore (Eds.), *Research in organizational change and development*. Greenwich, CT: JAI Press.

Manz, C. C., & Neck, C. P. (1999). *Mastering self-leadership: Empowering yourself for personal excellence, (Second edition)*. Upper Saddle River, NJ: Prentice Hall.

Manz, C. C., & Neck, C. P. (2004). *Mastering self-leadership: Empowering yourself for personal excellence*, (Third edition). Upper Saddle River, NJ: Pearson Prentice-Hall.

Manz, C. C., & Sims, H. P., Jr. (1980). Self-management as a substitute for leadership: A social learning theory perspective. *Academy of Management Review, 5*(3), 361–367.

Manz, C. C., & Sims, H. P., Jr. (1987). Leading workers to lead themselves: The external leadership of self-managing work teams. *Administrative Science Quarterly, 32*(1), 106–128.

Manz, C. C., & Sims, H. P., Jr. (2001). *New superleadership: Leading others to lead themselves*, San Francisco, CA: Berrett-Koehler.

Maslach, C., Jackson, S., & Leiter, M. P. (1996). *Maslach burnout inventory* (3ʳᵈ ed.). Palo Alto, CA: Consulting Psychologists Press.

Maslach, C., & Leiter, M. P. (1997). *The truth about burnout.* San Francisco, CA: Jossey Bass.

McClelland, D. C., Atkinson, J. W., Clark, R. W., & Lowell, E. L. (1953). *The achievement motive.* New York: Appleton-Century-Crofts.

McCrae, R. R., & John, O. P. (1992). An introduction to the 5-factor model and its applications. *Journal of Personality, 60*(2), 175–215.

Meindl, J. R., Ehrlich, S. B., & Dukerich, J. M. (1985). The romance of leadership. *Administrative Science Quarterly, 30*(1), 78–102.

Motowidlo, S. J., Borman, W. C., & Schmit, M. J. (1997). A theory of individual differences in task and contextual performance. *Human Performance, 10*(2), 71–83.

Murphy, S. E., & Ensher, E. A. (2001). The role of mentoring support and self-management strategies on reported career outcomes. *Journal of Career Development, 27*(4), 229–246.

Neck, C. P., & Houghton, J. D. (2006). Two decades of self-leadership theory and research: Past developments, present trends, and future possibilities. *Journal of Managerial Psychology, 21*(4), 270–295.

Neck, C. P., & Manz, C. C. (1992). Thought self-leadership: The influence of self-talk and mental imagery on performance. *Journal of Organizational Behavior, 13*(7), 681–699.

Neck, C. P., & Manz, C. C. (1996). Thought self-leadership: The impact of mental strategies training on employee cognition, behavior, and affect. *Journal of Organizational Behavior, 17*(5), 445–467.

Neck, C. P., & Manz, C. C. (2010). *Mastering self-leadership: Empowering yourself for personal excellence* (5ᵗʰ ed.). Upper Saddle River, NJ: Pearson Prentice Hall.

Nel, P., & Van Zyl, E. (2015). Assessing the psychometric properties of the revised and abbreviated self-leadership questionnaires. *SA Journal of Human Resource Management, 13*(1). doi: 10.4102/sajhrm.v13i1.661.

Norris, S. E. (2008). An examination of self-leadership. *Emerging Leadership Journeys, 1*(2), 43–61.

Oliveira, L. B. D., & Silva, F. F. R. A. (2015). The effects of high performance work systems and leader member exchange quality on employee engagement: Evidence from a Brazilian non-profit organization. *Procedia Computer Science, 55*(2015), 1023–1030.

Organ, D. W. (1988). *Organizational citizenship behavior: The good soldier syndrome.* Lexington, MA: Lexington Books.

Park, J., Yun, E., & Han, S. (2009). Factors influencing nurses' organizational citizenship behavior. *Journal of Korean Academician Nursing, 39,* 499–507.

Park, W. Y., & Yoon, S. H. (2009). The mediating role of OCB between organizational justice and organizational effectiveness in nursing organizations. *Journal of Korean Academy of Nursing, 39*(2), 229–230.

Park, Y. K., Song, J. H., & Lim, S. D. (2016). Organizational justice and work engagement: The mediating effect of self-leadership. *Leadership & Organization Development Journal, 37*(6), 711–729.

Parker, S. K. (1998). Role breadth self-efficacy: Relationship with work enrichment and other organizational practices. *Journal of Applied Psychology, 83*(6), 835–852.

Pearce, C. L., & Manz, C. C. (2005). The new silver bullets of leadership: The importance of self- and shared leadership in knowledge work. *Organizational Dynamics, 34*(2), 130–140.

Penner, L. A., Midili, A. R., & Kegelmeyer, J. (1997). Beyond job attitudes: A personality and social psychology perspective on the causes of organizational citizenship behavior. *Human Performance, 10*(2), 111–131.

Peter, J. P. (1981). Construct validity: A review of basic issues and marketing practices. *Journal of Marketing Research, 18*(2), 133–145.

Pfeffer, J. (1994). *Competitive advantage through people.* Boston, MA: Harvard Business School Press.

Pfeffer, J. (1998). Seven practices of successful organizations. *California Management Review, 40*(2), 96–124.

Plessis, Y. D., & Barkhuizen, N. (2011). Psychological capital: A requisite for organizational performance in South Africa. *South African Journal of Economic and Management Sciences, 15*(1), 16–30.

Pongpearchan, P. (2016). Effect of transformational leadership and high performance work system on job motivation and task performance: Empirical evidence from business schools of Thailand universities. *Journal of Business and Retail Management Research (JBRMR), 10*(3), 93–105.

Prussia, G. E., Anderson, J. S., & Manz, C. C. (1998). Self-leadership and performance outcomes: The mediating influence of self-efficacy. *Journal of Organizational Behavior, 19*(5), 523–538.

Qadeer, F., & Jaffery, H. (2014). Mediation of psychological capital between organizational climate and organizational citizenship behavior. *Pakistan Journal of Commerce and Social Sciences, 8*(2), 453–470.

Raykov, T., & Marcoulides, G. A. (2011). *Introduction to psychometric theory.* New York: Taylor & Francis.

Richer, S. F., Blanchard, C., & Vallerand, R. J. (2002). A motivational model of work turnover. *Journal of Applied Social Psychology, 32*(10), 2089–2113.

Rioux, S. M., & Penner, L. A. (2001). The causes of organizational citizenship behavior: A motivational analysis. *Journal of Applied Psychology, 86,* 1306–1314.

Roberts, D. R., & O'Davenport, T. O. (2002). Job engagement: Why it's important and how to improve it. *Employment Relations Today, 29*(3), 21–29.

Ryan, R. M., & Deci, E. L. (2000). Self-determination theory and the facilitation of intrinsic motivation, social development, and well-being. *American Psychologist, 55*(1), 68–78.

Ryan, R. M., & Deci, E. L. (2007). Active human nature: Self-determination theory and the promotion and maintenance of sport, exercise, and health. In M. S. Hagger & N. L. D. Chatzisarantis (Eds.), *Intrinsic motivation and self-determination in exercise and sport* (pp. 1–19). Champaign, IL: Human Kinetics.

Saks, A. M., & Ashforth, B. E. (1997). A longitudinal investigation of the relationships between job information sources: Applicant perceptions of fit, and work outcomes. *Personnel Psychology, 50*(2), 395–426.

Satterfield, D. W., & Davidson, J. K. (2000). Integrated team approaches to self-management education, care and evaluation. In J. K. Davidson (Ed.), *Clinical diabetes mellitus: A problem oriented approach* (pp. 219–232). New York: Thieme.

Schaufeli, W. B., & Bakker, A. B. (2003). Utrecht Work Engagement Scale Preliminary Manual, Version 1. Retrieved from http://www.wilmarschaufeli.nl/publications/Schaufeli/Test%20Manuals/Test_manual_UWES_English.pdf.

Schaufeli, W. B., Salanova, M., Gonzalez-Roma, V., & Bakker, A. B. (2002). The measurement of engagement and burnout: A two sample confirmatory factor analytic approach. *Journal of Happiness Studies, 3*(1), 71–92.

Schwarzer, R., & Jerusalem, M. (1995). Generalized Self-Efficacy scale. In J. Weinman, S. Wright, & M. Johnston (Eds.), *Measures in health psychology: A user's portfolio. Causal and control beliefs* (pp. 35–37). Windsor, UK: Nfer Nelson.

Seibert, S. E., Silver, S. R., & Randolph, W. A. (2004). Taking empowerment to the next level: A multiple level model of empowerment, performance, and satisfaction. *Academy of Management Journal, 47*(3), 332–349.

Shalley, C. E., Zhou, J., & Oldham, G. R. (2004). The effects of personal and contextual characteristics on creativity: Where should we go from here? *Journal of Management, 30*(6), 933–958.

Snell, S. A. (1992). Control theory in strategic human resource management: The mediating effect of administrative information. *Academy of Management Journal, 35*(2), 292–327.

Stajkovic, A. D., & Luthans, F. (1988). Self-efficacy and work-related performance: A meta-analysis. *Psychological Bulletin, 124*(2), 240–261.

Stewart, G. L., Carson, K. P., & Cardy, R. L. (1996). The joint effects of conscientiousness and self-leadership training on self-directed behavior in a service setting. *Personnel Psychology, 49*(1), 143–164.

Stewart, G. L., Courtright, S. H., & Manz C. C. (2011). Self-leadership: A multi-level review. *Journal of Management, 37*(1), 185–222.

Streiner, D. L., Norman G. R., & Cairney, J. (2015). *Health measurement scales: A practical guide to their development and use.* Oxford, UK: Oxford University Press.

Sun, L., Aryee, S., & Law, K. (2007). High-performance human resource practices, citizenship behavior and organizational performance: A relational perspective. *Academy of Management Journal, 50*(3), 558–577.

Tabak, A., Sığrı, Ü., & Türköz, T. (2009). Öz liderlik (Kendi kendine liderlik) ölçeği Türkçe formunun uyarlama çalışması. *17. Ulusal Yönetim ve Organizasyon Kongresi,* (pp. 303–309). Eskişehir, Turkey: Osmangazi Üniversitesi.

Takeuchi, R., Lepak, D. P., Wang, H., & Takeuchi, K. (2007). An empirical examination of the mechanisms mediating between high-performance work systems and the performance of Japanese organizations. *Journal of Applied Psychology, 92*(4), 1069–1083.

Thoresen, C. E., & Mahoney, M. J. (1974). *Behavioral self-control.* New York: Holt, Rinehart & Winston.

Tomer, J. F. (2001). Understanding high performance work systems: The joint contribution of economics and human resource management. *Journal of Socio-Economics, 30*(1), 63–73.

Trahant, B. (2007). Debunking five myths concerning employee engagement: A recent report debunks the myths and reveals practices for enhancing individual employee effectiveness to improve organizational performance. *Public Management, 36*(1), 53–60.

Tuckey, M. R., Bakker, A. B., & Dollard, M. F. (2012). Empowering leaders optimize working conditions for engagement: A multilevel study. *Journal of Occupational Health Psychology, 17*(1), 15–27.

Turgut, T., & Erden, N. (2013). Olumsuz test ifadelerinin iç tutarlılığa ve faktör yapısına etkileri. *İstanbul Üniversitesi İşletme Fakültesi Dergisi, 2*(42), 319–332.

Tyler, T. R., & Blader, S. L. (2000). *Cooperation in groups: Procedural justice, social identity and behavioral engagement.* Philadelphia, PA: Psychology Press.

Uhl-Bien, M., & Graen, G. B. (1998). Individual self-management: Analysis of professionals' self-managing activities in functional and cross-functional teams. *Academy of Management Journal, 41*(3), 340–350.

Ullman, J. B. (2001). Structural equation modeling. In B. G. Tabachnick & L. S. Fidell (Eds.), *Using multivariate statistics* (pp. 653–771). Needham Heights, MA: Allyn & Bacon.

Unsworth, K. L., & Mason, C. M. (2012). Help yourself: The mechanisms through which a self-leadership intervention influences strain. *Journal of Occupational Health Psychology*, *17*(2), 235–245.

Vansteenkiste, M., Simons, J., Lens, W., Sheldon, K. M., & Deci, E. L. (2004). Motivating learning, performance, and persistence: The synergistic effects of intrinsic goal contents and autonomy-supportive contexts. *Journal of Personality and Social Psychology*, *87*(2), 246–260.

Viney, W., & King, D. B. (1998). *A history of psychology: Ideas and context*. Boston, MA: Allyn and Bacon.

Wang, J. H. Y., & Guthrie, J. T. (2004). Modeling the effects of intrinsic motivation, extrinsic motivation, amount of reading achievement on text comprehension between US and Chinese Student. *Reading Research Quarterly*, *39*(2), 162–186.

Williams, L. J., & Anderson, S. E. (1991). Job satisfaction and organizational commitment as predictors of organizational citizenship and in-role behaviors. *Journal of Management*, *17*(3), 601–617.

Williams, S. (1997). Personality and self-leadership. *Human Resource Management Review*, *7*(2), 139–155.

Wood, S., & Wall, T. D. (2002). Human resource management and business performance. In P. Warr (Ed.), *Psychology at work* (pp. 351–374). London, UK: Penguin.

Wood, S. J., Stride, C. B., Wall, T. D., & Clegg, C. W. (2004). Revisiting the use and effectiveness of modern management practices. *Human Factors and Ergonomics in Manufacturing & Service Industries*, *14*(4), 415–432.

Wu, C., & Wang, Y. (2011). Understanding proactive leadership. In W. H. Mobley, M. Li, & Y. Wang (Eds.), *Advances in global leadership* (pp. 299–313). Bingley, UK: Emerald.

Xanthopoulou, D., Bakker, A. B., Demerouti, E., & Schaufeli, W. B. (2007). The role of personal resources in the job demands-resources model. *International Journal of Stress Management*, *14*(2), 121–141.